1620.
1726. KINGSTON. 1876
1776.

REPORT

OF THE

PROCEEDINGS AND EXERCISES

AT THE

ONE HUNDRED AND FIFTIETH

ANNIVERSARY

OF THE

INCORPORATION OF THE TOWN OF KINGSTON, MASS.

JUNE 27, 1876.

BOSTON:
E. B. STILLINGS & CO., PRINTERS,
15 SPRING LANE.
1876.

OFFICERS OF THE DAY.

President.
NATHANIEL ADAMS, ESQ., OF BOSTON.

Vice-Presidents.

HON. JOSEPH R. CHANDLER,	Penn.	WILLIAM R. SEVER, ESQ.	Mass.
HON. GEORGE B. HOLMES,	R. I.	REV. JOB WASHBURN,	Me.
HON. EDWARD S. TOBEY,	Mass.	REV. WILLIAM A. DREW,	"
RUFUS R. COOK, ESQ.,	"	DR. C. C. HOLMES,	Mass.
HON. GEORGE G. LOBDELL,	Del.	HON. HENRY S. WASHBURN,	"
HON. FRANCIS M. JOHNSON,	Mass.	HENRY R. GLOVER, ESQ.,	"
DR. FRED. W. BARTLETT,	N. Y.	PHILIP HOLMES, ESQ.,	Me.
REV. WINSLOW W. SEVER,	"	PROF. ALBERT STETSON,	Ill.
THOMAS D. STETSON, ESQ.,	"	JAMES B. STETSON, ESQ,	Cal.

Chief Marshal . . . . CORNELIUS A. FAUNCE.

Aids.

CYRUS W. RIPLEY.	LEWIS H. KEITH.
QUINCY A. FAUNCE.	WALTER H. FAUNCE.

Chaplain . . . . REV. JOSEPH PECKHAM.
Toast-Master . . . . W. R. ELLIS.

Executive Committee.

KIMBALL W. STETSON, *Chairman.*
And Chairman of Committee on Invitations and Correspondence.

WALTER H. FAUNCE, *Secretary.*   HORATIO ADAMS, *Treasurer.*

HENRY K. KEITH	*Chairman of Committee on Reception.*
JAMES H. DAWES	" " Tents.
CALEB BATES	" " Fireworks.
AZEL H. SAMPSON	" " Finance.
WILLIAM H. BURGES . . .	" " Public Dinner.
PHILANDER COBB	" " Music.
CORNELIUS A. FAUNCE . . .	" " Music.
LEWIS H. KEITH	" " Decorations.
CYRUS W. RIPLEY	" " Military.
FRANK H. FULLER	" " Ringing of Bells.

Committee of Publication.

JOSEPH PECKHAM,   WALTER H. FAUNCE,
HORATIO ADAMS.

INTRODUCTION.

The one hundred and fiftieth anniversary of the incorporation of Kingston, coming only one week before the centennial birthday of the nation of which it forms a small but not unimportant part, the question began frequently to be asked both by present and past citizens, Why not unite in a commemoration of the day? The desirableness of this appeared all the greater, since nothing of the kind was known ever to have occurred, and since the materials for a town history, even from the landing of the forefathers, when Kingston was a part of Plymouth, had been largely gathered and only needed to be brought before the public to give to the occasion an extraordinary interest. The special appropriateness of a celebration at this time was further evinced by the proclamation of the President of the United States, in accordance with an Act of Congress, inviting the people throughout the country to assemble in their respective municipalities on the 4th of July, to recount their local histories, and then to deposit copies of the same in the public archives at Washington. This centennial year has not only given greater intensity to the passion of antiquarians for collecting every pamphlet and paragraph, every name and date, that pertain in any way to the local annals, but also has awakened a universal curiosity in all matters of the past. From year to year, increasing efforts are bestowed upon historical and genealogical research and greater pains are taken for the preservation of the perishable records and fading traditions of the first settlements.

It was evidently no less the duty than the honest pride of a town, so rich in Pilgrim and Revolutionary memorials as Kingston, to contribute its important share to the historic treasures of the country.

In compliance with this awakened interest, several notices were posted in different public places of the town inviting the citizens to meet at the Town Hall on the evening of April 25, 1876, "for the purpose of adopting such measures as they might deem desirable." As the result, it was unanimously voted to celebrate. The business of the preparation was distributed among ten different committees, the chairmen of which were to have the general oversight and were to constitute the Executive Committee. The committees thus organized proceeded at once to their several duties with a zeal and efficiency that meant success. The interest daily increased through the whole community, till those who were indifferent or opposed at first vied with the foremost in contributing to the material aid and to the pleasures of the occasion. Including the expense of the public dinner, more than fifteen hundred dollars were readily raised by voluntary gifts.

The services of a first-class brass band (the South Abington) to discourse the music, and of the oldest military company under the charter of the State (the Halifax Light Infantry) to perform the escort, were secured. This military company was organized in 1792. Under the first call of President Lincoln for troops, after the firing upon Fort Sumter, its captain (Harlow), receiving the summons at midnight, warned every member thereof, though residing in seven different towns, so that without exception they took the earliest train the next morning on their way to the scene of conflict. The last act of this gallant company before being disbanded was the escort duty most acceptably performed at our anniversary.

INTRODUCTION.

The Commi tee on Invitations and Correspondence, after much painstaking, particularly of one of their number,* collected and registered in a book for the purpose nearly six hundred names of former residents of the town, and of those otherwise connected with it, belonging to twenty-seven different States of the Union, to each of whom, by private hand or through the mail, they sent a handsomely printed circular cordially inviting them all and severally to revisit on this natal, festal day the old home, and assuring them that it would be an occasion for many pleasant reunions and reminiscences. That none might by any possibility be omitted, notices of the contemplated celebration, and invitations thereto were published in various newspapers. The responses of the sons and daughters of Kingston residing in these different portions of the land proved conclusively, that a deep chord had been touched in their hearts, and we were sure of a large gathering. Where there were such numbers of the distinguished sons, worthy of official prominence and well qualified to entertain the audience on such an occasion with speech, it became a somewhat delicate and painful duty of the Executive Committee to set narrow limits and to give the positions of honor only to a few representatives of the different families and States.

The place selected for the main services was Thomas's Hill, being a part of the estate of Gen. John Thomas, of Revolutionary memory, and commanding a view of the bay where the Mayflower was moored, of the island where the Pilgrims, under the canopy of a wintry sky, "rested the first Sabbath," of the hill at whose base their valiant captain resided, and of the river, winding through our territory, named for the captain of the Mayflower, and on whose borders the Pilgrims " had a great liking to plant." Within a few rods of this hallowed spot,

* Mr. Cornelius A. Bartlett.

the last survivor of the Mayflower passengers, Mary Allerton, relict of Elder Thomas Cushman, expired, and from this mount of vision could be easily discovered, within the limits of what is now Kingston, the localities where dwelt the Bradfords, Gov. Thomas Prence, Allerton and Cushman, Fuller, Howland, and Cooke, Paddy and Willett; also the lands of numerous others who were among the early comers. In 1838 this hill was selected by the artist of Barber's *Historical Collections of Massachusetts* as presenting the most favorable view of the pleasant village with its churches and surroundings; and it is certain that the progress of nearly forty years since that date, has been continually adding to the landscape in every direction the charms of trim shrubberies, of graceful lawns, and handsome structures.

Providentially the 27th of June, though sharing somewhat largely in the heats of the summer solstice, was yet one of the loveliest, balmiest, and most comfortable days of that pure, leafy, and rosy month. The echoes of the morning were awakened by the ringing of the church-bells and the firing of cannon and anvils, and there was a repetition of the firing and ringing at sunset. "The Antiques and Horribles" including a goodly number who personated the dusky aborigines, thus carrying the imagination back into the remote and misty past, glided through the streets in the early morn, and soon were seen no more. It is not the province of the prosaic journalist or historian of a day, to record the transactions of the unseen world, but he would be regarded as very unimpressible and stupid indeed, not to allow that, at least on a day like this, the venerable fathers were invisibly present as deeply interested spectators.

Precisely at nine o'clock at the sound of fife and drum, a preliminary procession, consisting of the children of the public schools and citizens, under the direction of the efficient marshal and his aids, took up the line of march from the Town Hall for the Old Colony Station to receive the invited guests. In a brief time after the arrival of the cars the procession was greatly enlarged, and was re-formed in the following order: —

Bowle's South Abington Band, with twenty pieces.

Halifax Light Infantry under command of Capt. Geo. H. Bonney, Jr. of this town, with forty-seven muskets.

Governor's staff and Secretary of State.

President of the day.

Vice-Presidents.

Orator, Historian, and Poet.

Other Invited Guests.

Aged men and women of the town.

High, Grammar, and Primary Schools.

Citizens.

Nearly one hundred carriages passed at a given point near the depot, while the number of persons on foot was uncounted. The procession moved first to the estate formerly owned by Gov. Bradford and his almost equally illustrious son, William Bradford, Jr.; passing the cellar of the house occupied at least by the latter, and also by the last apple-tree of his orchard, a high-top sweeting, set out, it is believed, in 1669, and which in this year of grace 1876 bears a small quantity of fair fruit; then returning by the depot and Town Hall, it passed through the main street to the Hill. Most of the dwellings on the route were handsomely and some even elegantly decorated with flags and streamers, with ensigns and shields, with evergreens and flowers, while the older edifices were marked with mottoes indicative of the times when built and of various historical associations. The national emblem with its stars and stripes floated from numerous liberty poles, erected by private enterprise, and at all favorable points was suspended across the streets. The whole village put on a gala-day dress, and seemingly the entire population, with hundreds from the neighboring towns, were gathered to mingle in the festivities. "Upon the lawns and ornamented spots about the dwellings passed by the procession, the ladies had collected, and saluted it by the waving of handkerchiefs and such demonstrations as their enthusiasm prompted, rendering the scene more animated and greatly adding to the prevailing good feeling." The occasional hearty hand-shaking, when two aged ones met and recognized in each other the boy or girl of their youthful pastimes and school-days, formed one of the most touching spectacles of the occasion. The ancient town was rejuvenated and the oldest present seemed among the youngest. Notwithstanding the crowds, not an instance of intoxication or disorder occurred to disturb the public ceremonies and exercises of the day, nor was there the slightest accident to mar the universal pleasure.

The procession having arrived at the spacious pavilion at the end of the route, the president, other officers, and guests were marshalled to the platform, in the rear of which were the names conspicuously posted of the first four ministers of the town, Stacey, Maccarty, Rand, and Willis, with the dates of their pastorates, and also the motto, reaching quite across the tent, "Our Fathers' God hath prospered us." Directly in front of the speakers' stand were seated, as the representatives of a former generation, some twenty Kingston octogenarians, while from 1,500 to 2,000 people were either seated under the canvas or stood within hearing distance.

Promptly at eleven o'clock the exercises began with an address of welcome from the president of the day as follows:—

SPEECH OF NATHANIEL ADAMS.

Ladies and Gentlemen, Fellow Town-people,—I have been delegated by your Executive Committee to extend to you, one and all, a sincere, hearty welcome to this the one hundred and fiftieth anniversary of the incorporation of this place as the town of Kingston, and to assure you that all the preparations and arrangements have been made for your especial enjoyment.

The occasion is well calculated to renew in our minds that respect and veneration we owe to our ancestors, who, one hundred and fifty years ago, laid the foundation of what we see in Kingston to-day, and to revive in our memories the days of our childhood and of our school-days. The occasion will afford a rare opportunity to exercise that social element of our nature with which our Creator has so liberally endowed us all, and it is hoped that all will avail themselves of this favorable opportunity. The causes and reasons which actuated our ancestors in petitioning for the incorporation of the town, and the success of their descendants in maintaining it, down to the present time, will be related to you by the historian and orator of the day.

I have been introduced by your marshal in a very happy manner, and yet I am none other than one of those Adams boys who left this ancient town at the age of seventeen, about forty-seven years ago, a little older to be sure, and have been a resident of the city since that time. I am greatly indebted to this town for its many influences for good.

I remember well my senior townsmen, many of whom have

gone to their great reward. I remember their generous and encouraging words intended for my guidance; words which, if not strictly heeded, have never been forgotten.

I am indebted to this town for other circumstances in early life. I had the honor of graduating at the age of sixteen, from a seminary supported by this town, called Crossman Pond School. The most of my preparation before entering that seminary was obtained from Mrs. Abigail Foster, a lady well calculated to impart her knowledge to the lads and misses of her day. The principal of that seminary at the time I graduated was Samuel Ring, Esq., a gentleman I remember with respect. I well remember his parting address to the graduating class, and some of the possibilities he hoped we might attain unto; but alas! the most prominent of them is OLD AGE.

The exercises of the occasion will now commence.

Immediately after this address a selection from the Scriptures was read by Rev. C. Y. DeNormandie, and a prayer was offered by the Chaplain of the day. The following original hymn, composed by Dr. T. B. Drew, was then sung by the audience, accompanied by the band, to the tune of America:—

HYMN.

We gather here this hour,
On us thy blessings shower,
   Father divine!
And while we mingle here
This first "Centennial Year,"
We feel thy presence near,
   The glory thine.

A century has gone
Since "Freedom's land" was born
   'Mid hopes and fears;
But ere that glorious day,
While Britain held her sway,
Kingston had sped her way
   Full fifty years.

And now our thoughts go back
O'er Time's well-beaten track,
    To those old days;
And ere it onward runs,
We'll think of sires and sons,
Mothers and loving ones,
    Who trod these ways.

Their pathway on in life
Led them to toil and strife
    And noble deeds,
And as their children see
The fruits of liberty,
May we true followers be,
    Where duty leads.

Our kindred! There they lie
Beneath this summer's sky,
    In yonder ground.
Where pain and sorrow cease,
There they at last found peace,
And all had sweet release
    In rest profound.

And as those paths we tread,
The ways our fathers led,
    Let us arise;
Press forward in our might,
And battle for the right,
Until we see the light
    Beyond the skies.

The other exercises of the morning were the oration by Rev. Joseph F. Lovering, of Watertown, the poem by George C. Burgess, Esq., of Portland, Me., and the historical sketch by Dr. Thomas B. Drew, of Plymouth, all natives of Kingston. These excellent and interesting productions, which were eloquently delivered, will be found in their appropriate places in the following pages.

At a quarter before two o'clock there was an adjournment, after half an hour's recess, to the mammoth dining-tent a few rods distant. The children of the schools had been provided with an entertainment in a separate tent, erected for the purpose. The seats for eight hundred and twenty-seven guests were all speedily occupied. The blessing of the God of the fathers, in a clear, firm voice, was now invoked by Rev. Job Washburn, of Camden, Me., the oldest person present, and probably the oldest living man, native of the town. Sharpened appetites gave additional relish to the bountiful repast prepared by Caterer Peirce, of Boston Highlands. Over twenty young ladies of Kingston, dressed in patriotic attire, "red, white, and blue," volunteered to wait upon the tables.

"After the battle of knives and forks was concluded," the President introduced the Toast-master. Numerous suggestive sentiments were successively presented, appropriate both to the occasion and to the several gentlemen expected to speak. Much to the regret of all, only a part of the toasts were responded to, for lack of time; but both the speeches that were actually delivered and most of those that would have been, will be found in the subsequent pages.

"The feast of reason," enlivened by many pleasant reminiscences of boyhood and former days, and by many coruscations of wit and eloquence had to be cut short, since one of the longest days of the year had sped too quickly in its exuberance of delights. It was appropriate that priority in the speaking should be chiefly given to the older men, to those who are the links connecting the town with its original founders, but it will certainly be right at the next centennial to give the first chance to those, if present, who were debarred the privilege at this.

The following hymn composed by Mrs. Caroline B. Burgess of Boston, a native of Kingston, was sung at the table.

INVOCATION HYMN.

Tune, "Italian Hymn."

Father Supreme, above,
Ruling in changeless love,
    Wisdom and power,
Thou who didst bow thine ear
Our fathers' prayer to hear,
Oh, graciously draw near,
    And bless this hour!

Thou who, with outstretched hand,
Didst guide the Pilgrim band
    Safe o'er the sea,
And gav'st them strength to bear
Hardship and want and care,
All ills content to share
    In serving thee,—

Their children scattered wide,
We pray thee guard and guide
    Through every ill.
On smooth or troubled sea,
With cheerful heart may we,
Trusting like them in thee,
    Obey thy will.

In us, O God, renew
The strength our fathers knew,
    And victory won!
Their patient courage lend,
Like grace and virtue send,
And every good descend
    From sire to son.

KINGSTON, June 27, 1876.

In the evening various choice pieces of music from the band, which had delighted all through the day, stirred the hearts of the multitude, while a fine display of fire-works gratified every beholder. As the concluding scene, apparently emblazoned upon a dark thunder-cloud which overhung the western horizon, and from which there were frequent flashes of pyrotechnics more grandly beautiful than those of art below, and as the fitting *finale* of a day more joyous, more fraternizing, fuller of delightful recollections and of happy anticipations than any other since the organization of the town, if not since its first settlement, there shone for several minutes, in letters of living light, awakening the echoing cheers of the witnessing throng, the royal name of the dear old town, with the dates of its beginning and of its present anniversary :—

1726. KINGSTON. 1876.

ORATION BY REV. JOSEPH F. LOVERING, WATERTOWN.

Mr. President, Fellow-citizens of Kingston, and Friends: — We celebrate to-day the one hundred and fiftieth anniversary of this town. We may do so with profound gratitude and exultation; for on this day we may take knowledge, not only of the immediate and detailed interests affecting this community throughout its history, but of those broader and more comprehensive relations that embrace the good fame of our noble commonwealth and the dignity and power of the nation. It may be said of every town, however restricted its territorial area, however small its census list, that it belongs not to itself alone but to the State. The mighty ocean, whose grand expanse stretches far away from these shores, lifts its majestic tides and fills the basins of Massachusetts and Plymouth Bays, sweeps round yonder Gurnet, and bears back the waters and overflows the channel of our Jones River with all its creeks and tributaries. Yet the mighty ocean welcomes not only the contributions of the Merrimac and Saco and Penobscot, and a host of larger and lesser rivers, but also the smaller gifts from the liquid veins of mountain torrents and meadow brooks. So, too, while the great life of a State bears up the fortunes of its constituent communities, and feeds with the pulse of its life the simpler and humbler activities of town and village, those communities themselves, however inconsiderable, nourish and sweeten and increase the life of the State. Tacitus in his Annals * very pertinently remarks: "*Pleraque eorum quæ ref-*

---
* Lib. IV, 32.

eram parva forsitan et levia memoratu videri, non nescius sum. Non tamen sine usu fuerit introspicere illæ, primo adspectu levia, ex quis magnarum sæpe rerum motus oriuntur."

"I am aware that many things to which I refer may seem trivial and not worth recording; yet it is not altogether useless to examine affairs which at first sight appear to be of no great account, since they often give rise to matters of large moment."

There is no need for us to urge any such consideration, however, as we invite attention to our goodly town. We have a direct and immediate interest in that inheritance of worth and influence which was born within the circuit of a half-dozen miles from here, when the vast extent of territory now embraced by this nation was a mighty wilderness. We boast a descent, however we have degenerated in individual instances, for we make no plea for personal desert, — let the next century and a half judge concerning that, — we boast, I repeat, of a descent which for elevation of motive, moral strength, matchless devotion to civil and religious principle, puts to shame the vaunted ancestry of kings; we have royal pedigree. For what better aristocracy can any land boast than the aristocracy of worth and intellect and valiant service? Such an aristocracy founded Plymouth colony, of which this town was most intimately and from the first a part, and made it forever honorable.

We cannot admire too greatly, we cannot honor too reverently our Pilgrim Fathers. Separating themselves from the tender associations of home and from the inheritance of social custom and churchly faith, on a pure question of personal morals and individual conviction, refusing to submit to any wrong which conscience recognized or to any ceremonial which reverence for God forbade, they expatriated themselves, they sought as exiles in a foreign land to cherish their love of virtue and adorn their spiritual faith, and when the way opened before them they did not hesitate under commandment of duty to tempt an untried ocean and an inclement season, that, under another sky and on virgin shores, they might construct a State whose compact should hold them to plain allegiance to simple integrity, personal rectitude, and a prosaic life, and enable them to build an altar, before which a clean conscience and a heartfelt devotion might bow in humble, thoughtful, consecrated worship. Plymouth Colony claims this high distinction that its enterprise started in the fear of God, and sought to establish itself on principles of righteousness and truth, — principles which, amid the blaze of hate, the whisperings of slander, or the storm of reproach, shall stand firm, enduring, eternal, as under the scorching heats of summer or the wild blasts of winter, and amid the angry surges of the ocean, shall stand that rock which, in 1620, was consecrated by the touch of Pilgrim feet.

It is well for us, at the invitation of such a day as this, to review the past. We stand upon an elevated table-land. From the summit of one hundred and fifty years we may look around us as from a hill of observation. Leave this village, with its shaded streets and quiet life, cross the bridge whose double arches span the Jones River, turn sharp to the right, bearing to the left after you have crossed a shallow trout-brook, and then follow the sandy road through thickets murmurous with insect life, through pine woods with the fragrance of balsam in their breath, skirting the shore of Smelt Pond, stopping a moment, if you please, to notice the easy, graceful sweep of an eagle that, startled from some resting-place, lifts himself on mighty pinions, as if he scorned the earth, into the blue of the heavens, and then, almost breaking your way through scrub-oak and birches and alder bushes, climb the narrow path whose sharp ascent brings you to the summit of

Monk's Hill. Now look about you! You turn almost instinctively to the ocean, but look landward. Far down into the valley, far away to the horizon, south and west, stretches for miles and miles an untravelled wilderness. It needs no extravagant fancy to imagine that thus it looked a hundred and fifty years ago. Whatever changes may have happened, from the woodman's axe or the besom of fire, it indicates sufficiently well the wilderness of long years ago. You see no indication of human life. There are shaded woods where the Indian to-day might live, and coverts where the timid deer may hide. With any thought of the past in our mind, we cannot fail to be impressed with its lonely and untamed solitude. Turn now so that the wilderness shall be at your back; look down the sloping sides of the noble hill, see the mirror-like brightness and beauty of the pond at its foot; then look beyond, far away across the broad, blue expanse of the level bay, till your eyes touch the bold headlands of Cape Cod, — the clenched fist on the forearm of Massachusetts, stretched out to hold back the mighty surges of the Atlantic, and to give to Massachusetts Bay and Plymouth harbor their first grand breakwater. Under the shelter of those headlands, within the security of that mighty arm, that compact for just and equal laws was written and subscribed for the "general" good and "in the name of God," by John Carver and his associates, Nov. 11, 1620, on board the Mayflower. The waves that break to-day upon these shores do not cease to echo the memory of that devoted company of God-fearing and heroic men and women.

This side the bay, you see the sharp, needle-like beach set before the town of Plymouth, which is itself veiled from our sight by the woodlands back of it. To the right are the pine-clad hills of Manomet; to the left, beyond the beach, the shores of the Gurnet; this side of it Saquish and Clarke's Island — the latter named after the mate of the Mayflower; still farther to the left is Captain's Point and the hill on which stands the monument erected to the memory of Miles Standish; between the shore at our feet and Captain's Hill we see the mouth of Jones River and can catch glimpses of the river as we follow it up till we see our beautiful village embowered in trees and admirably situated on a high and level plateau. If you look beyond our village you can catch glimpses of Duxbury and Marshfield and so follow the coast-line along, till turning to the north we see the range of Blue Hills in Milton and Dorchester.

A hundred years ago Monk's Hill was one of the beacon hills from which flashed the intelligence which, leaving the coast below, travelled by a well-defined series of beacon heights, till the Blue Hills brightened with their fires. Now we look over a peaceful country. The bay is whitened here and there with the sails of adventurous commerce. The land, in solitary homes and in clustering villages, gives indication of careful thrift and sober prosperity. From the wilderness at the back of us of one hundred and fifty years ago we may look from the hill of observation the present gives us, on scenes of comfort in multiplied homes and on the light of a future promise brighter and more cheerful than any beacon-fire of the past.

While we accept the sober worth of the present and its brilliant promise of a future with gratitude and exultation, we look back to the past with unfeigned admiration for its heroic fortitude and persistent energy. We cannot fail to notice the record it gives of facts which ennoble individual lives and indicate the majestic steps by which Divine Providence has led New England and the American people to the proud eminence occupied to-day.

I have referred already to the settlement of Plymouth. It is fitting we especially should keep it in mind. We can claim with peculiar appropriateness an inheritance in its wealth of renown. Some of the most respectable of the original colonists settled within the present limits of this town, such as Gov. Bradford, — or if that is disputed, certainly his son Major Bradford, at one time deputy governor of the colony, did live in the north part of the town, — Mr. Allerton, Dr. Fuller, Francis Cooke, Mr. Hanburg, Thomas Cushman, and others. Moreover at the very commencement of that settlement the project was entertained of making the site of this town the permanent locality for the colony. In *Bradford and Wilson's Journal** we read that the day after the landing of the Pilgrims, a company was sent out to view the land. "We found," says the Journal, "a creek, and went up three English miles, a very pleasant river at full sea." This river was our Jones River, so named from the master of the Mayflower. "This place," the Journal goes on to record, "we had a great liking to plant in, but it was so far from our fishing, our principal profit, and so encompassed with woods, that we should be in much danger of the salvages; and our number being so little, and so much ground to clear. So we thought good to quit and [not] clear that place till we were of more strength."

Fifteen years later, at the Colony Court held in March, persons were appointed "to confer on re-uniting with them at Duxborrow at Jones River, or at such place as shall be most convenient." Later in the same month, so the record informs us there was another meeting of the court and "after much conference about the neerer uniting of Plymouth and those on Duxborrough side, divers were appointed to view Jones his river and Morton's hole which were thought the fittest places and to

---

*See Young's Chronicles of the Pilgrims, Chap. 10.

render a reason for their judgment." The commission of conference thus authorized by the court consisted of five from Plymouth and five from Duxbury, and all but one met in council. They came to no unanimous conclusion, " seven of the said nine," says the record, " holding Jones River to be the fittest place for the uniting both places into a neerer society and there build a meeting-house and town. And the two preferred Morton's hole before Jones River. Afterwards the governor and council summoned said persons deputed as before had done and read their reasons of their judgement, and after long debating of the thing it was at length referred to the two churches on each side as churches to agree upon and end the same."* There is no record of any meeting of the churches " as churches," and so far as appears the whole matter was suffered to drop by mutual consent. It is thus evident, from the evidence cited, that this locality was prominently before the colony as a place for the principal and permanent settlement. Aside from any such consideration, however, we claim partnership in the renown which is so justly given to Plymouth, since it was not until nearly a century had past after the colony was founded that any separation took place between it and us. Social and civil rights, educational and religious privileges, were common to both. At last, in 1716, those living near Jones River took measures to secure an independent existence as a town. Their petition was not granted. Prominent and influential men were selected, however, to appear at the general court and advocate the cause of the petitioners, and one year later this place was set off as Jones River parish. For awhile this was satisfactory, but at last the people were aggrieved by unsuitable school and church accommodations, and after a good deal of earnest debate, commissioners were appointed to view the locality, and it was finally

*Old Col. Rec. Ct. orders I. 90.

decided that Jones River parish should be set off and incorporated as a town. This was in 1726. The first name proposed for the town was Asburton, but was not approved.* Lieut.-Gov. Dummer proposed Kingston, which was adopted.

The spirit of independence which led to the organization of the town was not peculiar. It was a legitimate expression of the principles advocated by the colony in its establishment, and it became common throughout the State. Indeed, the more we study succeeding events in the history of the country, the more important this town spirit will appear. We cannot emphasize too greatly its influence in encouraging and disciplining public patriotism. I ask your especial attention to it even at the risk of some repetition. We admire a river whose majestic current sweeps through the varying scenery of an extensive territory. The grand lines of a mountain are mirrored on its surface to-day, to-morrow the same waters glide sweetly through cultivated fields or picturesque woodlands; now it broadens into a lake peaceful as the blue heavens above it, and now restrains its flood till it shall wake the voice of the thunder as it pours its mighty volume over some Niagara height; now its smooth surface is so gentle that only a pastoral beauty slumbers in its embrace, and now it lifts up the freightage of a State, and bears a noble fleet upon its swelling bosom. Yet the river, deep and broad and strong as it may be, has been gathered out of country rivulets and from springs that have bubbled up under the cool shadows of distant forests. From such sources it feeds its tide. The sea may let its surges sound the praises of the river, but the river must sing in every wave the praises of the hills. After a similar fashion we judge the beneficence and authority of the State. The nation is strong in the union of the States, but each State receives the

*Mass. Hist. Coll. 2 Series, Vol. III, p. 168.

vital current of its strength from the separate towns and villages set upon the hill-tops or nestled in the valleys. This commonwealth is second to none in the nation. Its industry and valor, its enterprise and virtue, deserve our admiration and respect. He must be a degenerate son of Massachusetts who does not thank God that he can claim by birth or by adoption this noble old commonwealth as his home. There is no distinction more honorable than to have been born in Massachusetts, especially in that part of Massachusetts embraced by the old Plymouth Colony, and to be worthy of such birth. Yet the high estimation in which the State is to be held has been achieved by the independent spirit of the separate communities of which the State is composed. We cannot understand and appreciate the honorable and patriotic position Massachusetts held prior to and during the war of the Revolution without studying the character, the life, the fame of individual towns. It is not the province of this address even to review the causes, the complaints, the repeated aggravations which stirred up so much bitter controversy, so much personal recrimination and hatred, resulting in so long-continued and wasting a war as that of a hundred years ago. I simply desire you to take notice that the spirit which induced Kingston to demand independence as a town was the same spirit prevalent throughout all towns in all the colonies, and to take notice, also, that this same spirit made Kingston, as it made other towns, loyal to freedom, ready in support of public affairs, brave and resolute in opposition to the encroachments of the royalists. For this reason it had no sympathy with those who were satisfied with the British rule and desired to submit with slavish ignominy to British insults. For this reason this entire colony gave no unmistakable intimation to those who were disobedient to the high commandment of freedom and manhood that their absence would be more acceptable than their presence. A single instance will illustrate this better than any argument, and show the extreme feeling existing between the Tories and the Whigs, the first being the declared adherents of the crown, the other the vigorous defenders of American liberties. For it is to be remarked, we must look back of Lexington and Concord to greet the first movements of life that gave birth to American liberties. It is not enough to study the history of battle-fields, where the yeoman strength of our fathers met in open conflict with the hirelings of the British crown. You must look over the records of town life. There were indications of the coming struggle long months and years before the first angry blaze of a musket flashed its threat or the sound of a cannon echoed among our hills; Whigs and Tories were arrayed against each other; there were public controversies; there were acrimonious conflicts in social life. The large majority of Tories were outside Plymouth Colony. The same spirit which in religious matters made Plymouth Colony refuse to sign the circular* sent from the Massachusetts Colony, recommending capital punishment for worshipping God in a different form from their own, made Plymouth Colony almost unanimous in defence of civil liberty. Yet the following incident will show that they were sufficiently earnest in punishing what was deemed an infringement of social and civil rights. I give it as I find it in Sabine's *Loyalists of the American Revolution*. †

"Jesse Dunbar, of Halifax, bought some cattle of a mandamus councillor in 1774 and drove them to Plymouth for sale. The Whigs soon learned with whom Dunbar had presumed to deal, and after he had slaughtered, skinned, and hung up one of the beasts, commenced punishing him for the offence. His

* Memorials of Marshfield, by Marcia A. Thomas, p. 47.
† Vol. I, Art. Jesse Dunbar.

tormentors, it appears, put the dead ox in a cart, and fixing Dunbar in his belly, carted him four miles, and required him to pay one dollar for the ride. He then was delivered over to a Kingston mob, who carted him four other miles, and exacted another dollar. A Duxbury mob then took him, and after beating him in the face with the creature's tripe, and endeavoring to cover his person with it, carried him to Councillor Thomas's house and compelled him to pay a further sum of money. Flinging his beef into the road, they now left him to recover and return as he could."

The hostility between Whigs and Tories was reported to be so wide-spread and bitter, notwithstanding order-loving people might have discountenanced any such expression of it, that Gen. Gage determined to send an armed force into the colony. This indignity was felt so sensibly and public sentiment was so greatly roused, that on Feb. 7, 1775, the selectmen of Kingston, in conjunction with those of Plymouth, Duxbury, Pembroke, Hanson, and Scituate signed a remonstrance protesting against it.* The Massachusetts Provisional Congress warmly approved of this procedure, and on the 15th of the month passed a special vote by which these towns were bidden, as the record reads, "steadily to persevere in the same line of conduct, which has, in this instance, so justly entitled them to the esteem of their countrymen; and to keep a watchful eye upon the behavior of those who are aiming at the destruction of our liberties."

Kingston did "persevere in the same line of conduct." She encouraged the loyal spirit already manifested, and prepared for the crisis which was near at hand. Some of her most prominent and energetic citizens, for instance, recruited a

* See Journal of Second Provincial Congress, under date Feb. 15, 1775.

company of minute men, commanded by Capt. Peleg Wadsworth, afterwards commissioned as general. The eager, devoted patriotism prevalent at that time throughout the colony, is well illustrated by an anecdote told of a member of a minute company, in a town originally embraced within the boundaries of Plymouth Colony. "In the front rank there was a young man, the son of a respectable farmer, and his only child. In marching from the village, as they passed his house, he came out to meet them. There was a momentary halt. The drum and fife paused for an instant. The father, suppressing a strong and evident emotion, said, 'God be with you all my friends! and, John, if you, my son, are called into battle, take care that you behave like a man, or else let me never see your face again.' The march was resumed, while a tear started into every eye." *

We need not go outside our own record, however, to catch the spirit of the times. We are honored to-day, in the person of our historian, with the presence of a great grandson of Seth Drew, who served as lieutenant of the company of Kingston men to which reference has been made. He was a ship-builder, and on the day when the news of the battle of Lexington reached the old colony, he was at work with his adze in the ship-yard. Without a moment's hesitation he called his brother James, gave his tools into his charge, and took his place in the ranks, and for more than eight years was prominently engaged in the war which gave us our nationality. At Roxbury during the battle of Bunker Hill, at Dorchester Heights when the British evacuated Boston, he served under the noble-hearted patriot and soldier, Gen. John Thomas. He was in the forefront of the battle at Saratoga when Burgoyne surrendered, and at Trenton, Monmouth, and on the Hudson River during that memora-

* Tudor's Life of Otis.

ble campaign. He was one of the court martial detailed to try Joshua Hett Smith as an accomplice of Major André, and in various services distinguished himself as a soldier and civilian. In the war of 1812 the Government appointed him to oversee the fortifications on the Gurnet and at Fairhaven and New Bedford. When the Society of the Cincinnati was formed he became a prominent member.* He was commissioned a Justice of the Peace, held the office for many years of postmaster and collector, and was deservedly esteemed by his fellow-citizens. He died at the advanced age of seventy-seven, in May, 1824.

There were other officers and men whose names are treasured in the annals of this town, such as Hezekiah Ripley, Crocker Sampson, and James Sever. The last named was a boy when the war broke out. At the close of the war in 1783 he was only twenty-two years old; yet he had won promotion, and held the honorable position of ensign, or of color-sergeant as that office is now called.

In such a spirit and by such men Kingston helped the cause of the Revolution. She furnished for the army, sixty men,† her full quota, contributed generously to the common supply. She gave under call of the Provincial Congress, convened at Watertown, May 31, 1775, thirty-eight coats as her proportion for the Massachusetts troops, and paid at one time more than $10,000 of the currency of the time for less than six months' service of a single soldier. In May, 1779, a committee was chosen "to examine the militia record and make a fair list of what services each person has done personally or by their

* In the history of this Society is this testimony to his character and worth: "Distinguished for activity of mind as well as of body, he sustained also the reputation of a brave and discreet officer, and merited and received the approbation and esteem of all with whom he associated."

† See Wm. T. Davis's Address, *Supra*.

money since June 1778." A list of such persons was reported, and the amount was as follows: —

	£	s	d
For the Continental service	267	3	4
For the secret expedition	177	0	0
For other purposes	73	10	0
Total	517	13	4

It may be well to state, in estimating the ten-thousand-dollar bounty referred to, that at one period a silver dollar would purchase one hundred in paper. Thacher, in his *History of Plymouth*, tells us that "a farmer sold a cow in the spring for $40 and in the next autumn paid the whole sum for a goose for Thanksgiving dinner."

In 1777 Kingston, together with Plymouth and Duxbury, built and manned a fort at the Gurnet. It is fitting I should mention another name which made the pages of our history brilliant during the Revolutionary War, — that of Gen. John Thomas. He was born in Marshfield in 1724, but after pursuing the study of medicine he settled in this town and is claimed among the number of her honored citizens. Our historian will, without doubt, make detailed reference to him. It is therefore unnecessary for me to say more than this, that he was held in high esteem not only by the people of this commonwealth, but throughout the colonies. He was so beloved by the army, so distinguished as a soldier, that he was honored by the personal solicitations of George Washington and Gen. Charles Lee and by special vote of the House of Representatives at Watertown, July 22, 1775, to induce him to retain his military command, notwithstanding he had been superseded, through the ill-advised action of the National Congress, by officers who had served under him. That action was rectified, and Gen. Thomas served to the satisfaction of all until his lamented death from small-pox in Canada, June 2, 1776.*

Such men as those I have named, such events as those suggested, may serve to indicate the temper of the times and the steadfast resolution which braced the people of these colonies to deeds of enduring renown. Let it be understood that we cannot measure the personality of any man by his immediate individual life, that we cannot describe or assign honor to any deed by simply comparing it, as it stands alone and at first, with other deeds acknowledged to be famous. The measure of a man is discovered in the influence he has upon his fellows, and in the inspiration his character and life give to succeeding generations; and the importance of a deed is to be told by its ultimate effect upon the destiny of a nation and the fortunes of a people. Under such law as this men like Thomas and Wadsworth and Drew and Sampson and others whose names are familiar in our annals are to be honored because they helped originate and increase and preserve that mighty spirit of loyalty to human rights and liberties, which, as the winds of heaven by the sceptre of their breath make forest trees bow before them, swayed the thoughts, fired the zeal, gathered up into heroic courage the hearts of men who followed their lead and wrought valiantly for God and the right. Under such law the mustering of a minute company in this town, the sharp decision that threw down the carpenter's adze, and said

---

*The nearest living descendant of Major-Gen. Thomas is Mr. Augustus Thomas, a native of Kingston. It is worthy of note that the use of the broad and open field where the exercises of the day occurred, from which there is an extensive view of the surrounding country and the harbor, was generously and courteously offered by Mr. Thomas to the Committee of Arrangements. In his green old age Mr. Thomas has the satisfaction of knowing that he has won and deserved the hearty respect of his fellow-townsmen.

farewell to home and peace and love, have a meaning as noble, because fraught with great results, as the gathering together of Cæsar's legions or Napoleon's battalions. It was because of the power of manhood back of the man himself and not to be determined by stature or speech; it was because of the power of manhood back of every squad of men, dressed in homespun and with flint-lock on their shoulders, however awkward it might be, that Lexington and Concord and Bunker Hill are names written high up upon the scroll that records deeds done in supreme consecration to liberty and justice for the cause of humanity and the service of God. And it was because this good town helped forward, by its manhood, that war of the Revolution in which renowned deeds were performed and in which such splendid heroism was illustrated, that it deserves our sincere and grateful veneration and applause.

In the succeeding history of the town I find nothing immediately affecting public affairs, unless I might except some earnest controversy about religious matters. The town pursued the even tenor of its way, sturdily attentive to its own concerns, ready by council and influence to assist the general weal. Between the Revolutionary War and that of 1812 there were built on an average about two hundred and fifty tons of shipping annually.* The war of 1812 was the most serious hindrance to its prosperity as it was to the general prosperity of the State. About thirty men enlisted from Kingston, most of whom were employed at the fortification on the Gurnet or in general coast-guard duty. Two only of the number survive, David Chandler and John Drew, known to you all as worthy and respected citizens. After the close of the war — at which time Kingston owned at the landing three sloops, one hundred and fifty tons; one brig, one hundred and sixty tons;

* Mass. Hist. Coll. 2 series, Vol. III.

at Rocky Nook six schooners, four hundred and forty-five tons, and two brigs, two hundred and fifty-six tons * — the modest, content, and sober life of the town continued as before, the most exciting topics being those connected with ordinary town affairs, questions affecting the election of town or state officers, or the conduct of the schools and the church, or the building of the railroad in 1845, which was as much of an event in my schoolboy days as the centennial celebration at Philadelphia is to the nation at large at the present time. It is a fact in which the residents of the town may well take commendable pride, that in social culture and general refinement and good morals Kingston occupies an enviable position. It will not be deemed an invidious comparison to say that no town within the limits of the old colony surpasses it in the strength of its integrity, in the fairness of its life, in its sustained though never extravagant enterprise, and in its praiseworthy thrift. The graceful purity of its homes bears testimony to the modest and beautiful lives of its mothers and daughters, and the vigorous, fair-minded character of its fathers and sons gives clear warrant of the continuance of its useful and honorable citizenship.

Nothing is now wanting to the compass of this address but a brief reference to the grand record which is given of the town during the war of the Rebellion. It was to be expected that every town in our beloved commonwealth would respond with ready patriotism to the call of the country's need. We look back through the years; we recall the days when the roll of the drum and the shrill notes of the fife were heard in the streets of every village along our shores and among our hills. The flash that glared from the cannon, pointed by rebel hands against the sacred honor and union of these States, represented as they were by Fort Sumter, served to light the beacon fires

* Mass. Hist. Coll. 2 series, Vol. III.

of unmatched and heroic patriotism on every Northern hill. The sullen threat of that cannon waked the echoes of loyalty in all our valleys, — echoes answered and repeated by the free surges of the Atlantic, as they break at the foot of Plymouth rock, and on every cliff along the shores of New England, while brave men, descendants of the minute-men of the Revolution, filled the ranks of volunteer regiments, and swore that the brave old flag, that had been torn down by treason and rebellion, should once again float on the free breeze of heaven, and be so firmly nailed by the strong right arm of the nation's manhood to every flag-staff and mast-head that never again should it be lowered to any foe at home or abroad. Thank God, the North kept its oath!

We greet to-day, in this company, those who fought for union and liberty, for country and humanity, those who are represented by the Kingston Boy, Capt. George H. Bonney, Jr., who is well worthy to command the gallant body of men from Halifax who do escort duty to-day. We greet to-day the grand old stars and stripes. We gather under the sacred shadows of its folds, and as we remember the past we renew our oaths that it shall float in beauty and strength over the whole country, North and South, East and West, and be honored of all nations on all seas from the rising to the setting sun.

Let it be the proudest boast of Kingston to-day that it was true to the record of the old colony and of the Revolution, that it helped crush the Rebellion and save the nation. It paid out of its town treasury $11,236.50; $5,574.08 were raised in addition by private subscription, making the whole amount raised and expended, exclusive of all State aid, $16,810.34, while at the close of the war it had cancelled all bills and held an available balance of $1,616.17. It may rightly boast, also, of its personal service. Shall it be said that we sent out none who commanded a position in these latter years equal to Thomas and Wadsworth and Drew in former years? If that is true, we sent out men who sustained nobly their own honor and that of their native or adopted town. Those men we salute to-day, — the one hundred and eighty-nine soldiers, "a surplus of nineteen over and above all demands," out of a population in 1865 of 1,626, — more than one in every nine; and with especial reverence we salute the memory of the heroic dead, the fourteen who died in service, one in every thirteen and a half of those who filled our quota.

> "Cheers, cheers for our heroes!
>   Not those who wore stars,
> Not those who wore eagles
>   And leaflets and bars.
> We know they were gallant,
>   And honor them, too,
> For bravely maintaining
>   The red, white, and blue.
>
> But cheers for our soldiers,
>   Rough, wrinkled, and brown, —
> The men who make heroes
>   And ask no renown.
> Unselfish, untiring,
>   Intrepid and true,
> The bulwark surrounding
>   The red, white, and blue."

The noble company of heroic men who represented this town in the army and navy of our country deserve our earnest gratitude and praise. They stood between their homes and the foe; they bared their breasts that the blows aimed at the life of the nation might strike them first; they helped form a living breast-work behind which the security and perpetuity of our country were safe. They deserved well of the republic. Let the names of the living be honored! Let the graves of the dead be the altars of our patriotism!

Pardon me, fellow-citizens, if I add a few words more. I said at the beginning of my address, and repeated in substance during it, that while the great life of a State bears up the life of its constituent communities, the communities themselves, however inconsiderable they may seem, nourish and sweeten and increase the life of the State. For our encouragement let this be emphasized. Town life has given the source from which the broader life of the State and the nation has been helped. De Tocqueville * says, "Municipal institutions, *i. e.*, towns and villages, are to liberty what primary schools are to science: they bring it within the people's reach, they teach men how to use and how to enjoy it." I need not attempt to prove to you the correctness of his statement. We know it to be true. In our government the township is the unit of power.

I wish, however, to remind you that aside from any direct and specific action, there are other methods by which the influence of a town is exerted. It is done not by the reputation the community may have at home, but by the character of those who go out from it, and are, as it were, its ambassadors. We must not neglect to acknowledge this, and to take pride in the meritorious and useful lives of those who love this town as the place of their nativity, and whose name, the town cherishes. No one will expect from me anything like a complete list of such persons. Many of you, however, recall the name of Joseph R. Chandler, member of Congress, minister to Naples, editor formerly of the *United States Gazette*, who lives in Philadelphia, venerable in years and in honor, and of Ichabod Washburn, late of Worcester, who bequeathed a fund for the relief of aged and indigent women in this town; of John Holmes, who was United States Senator from Maine, and of Dr. Ezekiel Holmes, teacher of Natural Sciences in the

* Democracy in America, Vol. I, Chap. 5.

same State; of Caleb Adams, of Brunswick, Me., who provided in his will for the establishment of a school in this town at some future time; of Rev. William A. Drew, formerly editor of the *Gospel Banner*, and Rev. Job Washburn, and of Samuel Adams, who invented the first reaping machine; of Edward S. Tobey, the successful merchant and efficient postmaster of Boston; of Francis M. Johnson of Newton, Henry Glover of Boston, and of many others who have enlarged the influence of this goodly town, last but not least of whom is William R. Sever, for so many years County Treasurer at Plymouth, and who can leave no better legacy for the rising generation than his spotless integrity, exact honesty, and clean moral worth. When a famous Grecian was asked what he could do, he replied, "I can make a little village into a populous city." His boast men like these I have named have made a fact. For greatness and power come not of size, but of brain and heart and hand.

Let us, then, with gratitude for the past and present, celebrate this one hundred and fiftieth anniversary of the incorporation of this town. Let us thank God for the mercy that has been so signally manifested to those who have preceded us, and let us pray that His favor may be with us, so that we may worthily endeavor to secure to our children a future which shall honor still more largely this beautiful and beloved town of Kingston.

POEM BY GEORGE C. BURGESS, ESQ., PORTLAND, ME.

STANDING upon this hill-top's grassy crown,
We look, with hearts aglow and eager, down
Upon the ocean, fields, and busy town.
    So from the summit of thrice fifty years,
    Backward we look, and plain to us appears
    The fabric which our memory uprears.
And as we look, the thronging visions come
Of those who made this fruitful spot their home.
We see the *rock* set in the salt-sea foam,
    Their shallop in the inner harbor rides,
    Stemming the rough waves of the winter's tides,
    While the swart savage from them lurking hides.
One hundred years! We see them stronger grown,
Their borders widen, fruitful seeds are sown,
They have made all the wilderness their own.
    In loyal homage to their well-loved king,
    The name of their new-founded town they bring,
    And KINGSTON call the accepted offering.
In fifty years how changed the feeling grows!
The land no king as earthly ruler knows,
Against all king-craft proving sturdy foes.
    One hundred more! How has the circle spread!
    There stands a *nation* in the *hamlet's* stead,
    And midst the proudest rears her wreath-crowned head.
As when the lightning flashes through the night,
One instant stands revealed to eager sight
A thousand forms of things distinct and bright,
    So memory's glance brings to our sight to day
    The forms of things though centuries away,
    To them I turn with my unskillful lay.

The scent of summer roses fills the air,
    Each summer bird trills now his sweetest lay,
And summer clouds hang low and languid where
    The quiet waters heave in yonder bay.
The growing corn waves in the Summer sun,
    And green fields stretch in peaceful length along;
Showing the fruits by sturdy labor won,
    Where Peace to Plenty sings her constant song.
Not so when first these shores our fathers trod,
    And sowed the seed which gave a nation life,

Building their altar in the name of God
    Where they might worship free from baneful strife.
Around them wildly raged the wintry blast,
    Before them spread an untrod wilderness,
Behind them lay a persecution past,
    Within them beat stout hearts of steadfastness.
What bitter grief those steadfast hearts did feel
    Who trod the level graves which hid their dead!
What sad forebodings visions drear did bring
    Filling their present with a nameless dread!
But never did their utmost longing trace
    A pathway backward crost the stormy main.
With fervent prayers they kept their hearts of grace,
    And trusted God to make their losses gain.
Their zeal and courage did so close them round,
    An atmosphere of life, that all within
The circle of their living, straightway found
    Themselves imbued with strength to theirs akin,
And children's children in the years that came
    Received from them a chrism of holy power,
A stern baptism, which kept them in the flame
    Of war's red breath and peril's deadly hour.
And these, though loving well the mother-land,
    Loved Freedom more, and with undaunted might
In bloody fields they took their lives in hand,
    Gave pledge to fortune, dared the unequal fight,
And with the priceless gift which Nature gave
    From sire to son, of courage joined to skill,
Scorned a luxurious ease if as a slave
    'T would be enjoyed; no rest they knew until,
The last fight o'er, the rights asserted won,
    The laurel wreath of victory on their brows,
A newer life with duties grave begun,
    To Freedom consecrate with holiest vows.
The choicest fruits which Victory gave they kept
    As noblest gifts for them by Heaven ordained;
And in their watch they slumbered not nor slept,
    Keeping the prize heroic courage gained.
Have we, their children, felt their spirits' fire,
    Their pride to do and dare, their holy zeal,
Their steady strength of will that did not tire,
    But self forgot in good of common weal?
We span the continent with iron bands,
    Pierce granite hills, and send the steam-urged steed
From Eastern shores to the far Western lands,
    Rivalling the sun in his resistless speed.

We stem the ocean's waves and river's tides
    With floating palaces, and even dare
The risk of life itself, where danger rides,
    To pierce the secrets of the upper air.
The words the Old World heard within the hour,
    And hearts that listened with warm rapture thrilled,
The quivering wire gives us with lightning's power
    Ere the applause which greeted them is stilled.
All that can minister to wealth or pride
    We dare and do; but in the nobler strife
Are our heart's promptings taken for our guide,
    To lead us upward to a higher life?
For us no forest spreads its trackless wild,
    For us no foes our peaceful homes molest;
No mother, trembling, watches o'er her child,
    Lest stealthy savage snatch him from her breast.
But other foes for other courage call,
    And other ills must anxious souls affright,
And who would not before their weapons fall
    Must with high courage watch and pray and fight.
How vain to us, dwelling upon the past,
    Seems in our sight this newer, later day!
How are our idols from their high seats cast,
    Their brazen fronts becoming crumbling clay!
The world, with stony visage, stands apart,
    And like the fabled sphinx a riddle tells
Which we must solve or die. As oft the heart
    Yields in despair as it in triumph swells;
The dusky smoke from almshouse and from jail
    Blots out the azure of the summer sky,
The cry of want and suffering's plaintive wail
    Is lost in the loud sound of revelry.
The swift gain not the race, nor do they win
    Amidst the battle's strife, the world calls strong,
Not always do they stand the assaults of sin
    Who in religion's armor have fought long.
And the clear ring of statesmen's voice we miss
    Who held their country as the all in all;
But now the chiefest statescraft comes to this, —
    To watch the means how parties rise and fall.
We praise our fathers' deeds, and hear with pride,
    Their noble story o'er and o'er retold;
Lest their example should our footsteps guide,
    We sell their landmarks in our greed for gold.
The stern, heroic soul, which every page
    Bears as the record of our fathers' lives,

Dwells not amongst us in this later age,
    And Honor's self with noblest purpose strives,
Full oft in vain, to win a poor success,
    Where fraud and swift deceit oppose the way,
And men get hearts of flint beneath the press
    Of the hard, shallow life we live to-day.
Oh, had we BRADFORD's stern integrity,
    Whose chosen path was of self-sacrifice,
Or CARVER's patient soul, whose loyalty
    To God and man was sealed at costliest price,
Or STANDISH's fiery zeal, whose ready hand
    Hurled mimic war wrapped up in serpent-skin,
Or BREWSTER's trust, who sought a foreign land,
    To holier lives his fellow-men to win!
But what our fathers did in that old time,
    Their sons who follow them must do to-day;
To loftier heights, with toiling feet, must climb,
    To purer air must urge our onward way;
Strive for the living faith to which they clung,
    Not to a dead belief nor blind assent,
Keeping our thoughts forever fresh and young,
    Our talents not as given but only lent.
'Gainst lust of office and the greed of trade,
    The loss of honor's quick, inspiring sense,
Placing our strength as walls of stone are made,
    To beat back ocean's waves of imminence.
So as from seed which in the ground is cast,
    And lifeless lies, forgotten, cold, and dead,
The future shall spring from the buried past,
    And wide abroad its living branches spread.

A brighter day is coming, and along the eastern sky
The crimson banners of the sun proclaim the dawn is nigh;
The purple tints of morning fade from off the topmost hills,
And a flood of radiance poured along the slumbering valleys fills.
The throbbing pulse of Mother Earth feels life awake anew,
And through the scattered clouds of night comes impulse strong and true.
Prophetic souls, with ears attent, hear a sound that stirs and cheers,
From future generations borne adown the coming years,
And midst the sound is heard no tramp of armed and mailed host,
War's trumpet-blast amidst the hum of Labor's throng is lost.
The shock of nations' angry jar shall vex nor land nor sea,
All nations, owning but one head, one brotherhood shall be;
The victories which Peace shall win shall far exceed the old,
Which War upon his battle-flags with pride hath oft enrolled;
Earth's stores for *all* her hapless sons shall then be garnered in,
Nor shall the strong against the weak in constant struggle win.

As 'neath the ocean's swelling flood the lightning bears amain
The message trusted to its care and swift returns again,
Obedient to the lightest touch the electric thrill is sent,
From zone to zone with speed untold, crost sea and continent,
So shall the world, with one accord responsive to the will
Of the great Master, cheerfully his purposes fulfil.
Upon Valhalla's open meads, the elder Eddas tell,
There stands the mystic tree of life, the ash-tree Ygdrasel.
Throughout the heavens its branches reach, and in the centre earth,
Deep as the mind can fathom depth, its secret roots have birth;
Upon its lofty topmost bough, with mighty spreading wings,
An eagle sits whose piercing gaze holds all created things.
The dew its branches all distill, its cool, protecting shade,
Give life to all, nor do they know if friends or foes they aid.
The gods who drink Hvergelmer's stream feel their full pulses swell,
The serpents gnawing at its roots are cherished too, as well.
The fountains springing from its roots are wit and wisdom's home,
And to their source at Mimer's fount the gods in judgment come.
There is no place unvisited, no lost, forgotten spot
The ash-tree's power has not searched out, though they may know it not.
Though long concealed, the hidden germ will yet be brought to life,
And, dead to mortal sight, is still with fruitful vigor rife.
The runes which Odin's hand has traced, this mystic sentence give,—
In the far twilight of the gods all better things shall live.
It needs not saga-lore the myth of Ygdrasel to read,
Nor which the mystic tree that grows upon the open mead.
That tree whose branches wide shall be throughout the broad heavens thrown,
Whose roots shall clasp the universe, is Freedom's tree alone.
Within its sheltering influence weak hearts are stronger made,
And even traitors claim their seats beneath its fostering shade.
And they who sought this spot remote, from home, from comfort turned
To breathe the air of freedom, all their vain allurements spurned.
Their bright example lives to day, and nations feel its might,
And turn towards it as the germ in growing seeks the light.
The murmur of the forest pines, the waves upon the shore,
And winds that blow at will shall bear the story evermore;
And full and strong the coming years shall see its ripened fruit,
Slow growing through the centuries, in every clime take root.
The chain from off the fettered limbs shall everywhere be riven,
The cry of anguish from the slave go up no more to heaven,
The mind in gloom of ignorance shall see the glorious light,
And Knowledge stand before mankind in radiant robes bedight,
Foul Superstition's baleful breath no more pollute the air,
And God's true spirit in his word find dwelling everywhere.
Oh, hasten on, thou glorious day, which brings upon the earth
The newer life, the freer soul, the nobler, purer birth!

HISTORICAL SKETCH, BY DR. T. B. DREW.

Sons and Daughters of Kingston: — For a long time I have had this day in anticipation. In 1856, at the suggestion of a friend, I commenced to collect whatever I could of an historical nature relating to Kingston, with a view of writing a history of the town at some future time. I knew then that 1876, besides being the centennial of our nation's birth, would also be the one hundred and fiftieth anniversary of the birthyear of our town, and the time then intervening was deemed fully sufficient to do any work of that kind at that day planned; yet the twenty years have passed away, and it is not accomplished.

But as you have chosen me the historian for this occasion, I have, with considerable labor, endeavored to select and condense from my material an historical sketch of that part of Plymouth which is now Kingston, from the earliest colonial times down to a period within the memory of persons still living, which, with your indulgence, I will now read: —

EARLY SETTLERS AND PROPRIETORS OF LANDS.

AT a very early period after the settlement at Plymouth by the Mayflower Pilgrims, A. D. 1620, and the division of lands, the colonists began to occupy their lots around the bay, so that after seventeen years only had elapsed (1637), a sufficient number to form a separate township had settled in that part of the town now Duxbury. About five years earlier a church had been formed there, causing, of course, a withdrawal of members from the Plymouth congregation. It was with great reluctance they were allowed to go, and to some minds it seemed that such divisions or separations would be a great disadvantage to the colony. They little realized that they were the founders of a great nation, and that such divisions must necessarily take place to form new settlements in other parts of New England. Gov. Bradford lamented these separations, and after expressing his feelings upon the subject, says, "*And this, I fear, will be the ruine of New England, at least of the churches of God there, and will provock the Lord's displeasure against them.*"

Could Bradford have looked into the future, he would have seen that New England itself would soon be too small to hold the descendants of those pioneers of the Plymouth and Massachusetts colonies, and he would have beheld them still pressing on through the western wilderness, until the shores of the Pacific were reached, three thousand miles away from the old rock on which they had landed two hundred and fifty years before. But we cannot wonder that, in those early days, they deeply felt those separations, especially in the church, and it is not strange some wished for a reunion. The question of uniting the Plymouth and Duxbury churches at Jones River was seriously discussed just previous to the incorporation of the latter town; but after a committee had reported favorably towards the project of building the meeting-house and town here, the matter was dropped. At this time just referred to, houses had been built and occupied in Rocky Nook and at Jones River, and I will now notice some of the principal persons who, previous to the year 1700, were residents or proprietors of lands in that part of Plymouth now Kingston.

The first ten or twelve whom I shall mention were either

Pilgrims on the Mayflower or arrived during the next year, 1621. Isaac Allerton was a very important man among the first comers, as he was almost at the head of their business affairs, and continued so until 1630, when his transactions, which at first had been profitable to them, proved in the end to be a loss, and many were involved, causing much unkind feeling towards him. He owned a house and farm at Rocky Nook, extending probably north to the river, embracing part of the estate of the late Alexander Holmes. Mr. Allerton went from Plymouth to New Amsterdam, and finally to New Haven, where he died about 1659.

William Bradford, the illustrious governor of Plymouth Colony, had a tract of land and a house at Stony Brook as early as 1637. Antiquarians have expressed doubts whether he ever lived so far from the town proper, but the following extracts from the records will seem to leave no doubt but that he resided in this part of the town, during portions of his life at least. In 1643, when he was governor, it was voted at a town meeting that "wolfe traps be made according to the order of court in manner following: 1st. That one trap be made at Jones River *by the governor's family*, Mr. Hanbury, and Mr. Prence and Matthew Fuller and Abraham Pierce." In 1644, when Winslow was governor, *Mr. Bradford's family at Jones River* was ordered "to furnish one person for a company in time of war or danger." Thus I see no reason for doubting that the governor lived here the two years last mentioned, if at no other time.

Francis Cook, the ancestor of the Cook family in this vicinity, lived at Rocky Nook. He was one of the first "layers out of land" in 1627, and died in 1663. His son John, who also came in the Mayflower when a child, lived at Rocky Nook. Another son, Jacob, who arrived shortly after the father, had lands near Smelt Brook. He was one of a number of soldiers who were "willing to goe upon service against the Pequent."

Clement Briggs owned land at Jones River and Rocky Nook previous to 1640.

Dr. Samuel Fuller, the first physician in the colony, had a house and farm at Rocky Nook, near Smelt Brook, although at the time of his death he dwelt in the town. He was a very valuable man in the colony, and in 1629, soon after the settlement at Salem, a general sickness prevailed there, and at the request of Mr. Endicott, Gov. Bradford sent him among them, which visit was greatly appreciated by the inhabitants of that new colony. In 1633 he himself fell a victim to an alarming sickness that prevailed at Plymouth, and died much lamented. From him the Fuller family here has descended.

John Howland had land at Jones River about 1638. The latter part of his life he dwelt at the Nook, northerly from the house of the late Hezekiah Ripley, where the remains of his cellar are still visible. He died in 1672.

Stephen Hopkins had a grant of land in the north meadow by Jones River in 1640. He was very prominent in public affairs, and died in 1644.

Elder Thomas Cushman resided on the farm at Rocky Nook that had previously belonged to his father-in-law, Mr. Allerton. The Elder's spring is still to be seen, and is one of the few ancient landmarks that can be pointed out to the present generation. From him the Cushman family in America is descended. His wife was Mary Allerton, who came a child in the Mayflower, and was the last survivor of the first-comers, dying in 1699, aged ninety. He died in 1691, aged eighty-four.

John Winslow, a brother of Gov. Winslow, had lands at Jones River before 1657.

As before stated, these persons I have noticed were of the earlier settlers, and now I will speak of prominent names of a later generation.

Major William Bradford, son of the governor, was one of the most important men in the colony. He resided at Stony Brook, probably in the same house that had belonged to his father, and the location of it can now be distinctly seen on the rising ground between the houses of Deacon Foster and the late Francis Drew. Persons now living in the neighborhood well recollect the old orchard that stood on the premises, and one tree still remains as a landmark of the past. Major Bradford was deputy governor from 1682 to 1686, and 1689 to 1692, when the colonial government terminated. Afterwards he was chosen a counsellor of Massachusetts.

In the year 1662, when Wamsutta or Alexander, the successor of Massasoit, was suspected of designs against the English, he was with Major Winslow when the chieftain was surprised and taken prisoner. The most eventful period of his life was during the years 1675–6, just two centuries ago. He was chief commander of the forces from Plymouth at the time King Philip and his people were attacked and routed from their stronghold in the Narragansett Swamp. The details of that bloody battle cannot be entered upon here. It is enough to say that on it seemed to depend the existence or destruction of the colonies. The English realized the situation, and in the depth of winter made one of the most desperate attacks on a savage foe that we find recorded in history. They gained the victory, but not without the loss of eighty men killed and one hundred and fifty wounded. In the year 1689 he is styled by the people of Rehoboth as the "Worshipful Major Bradford." Whether he was a member of the "secret fraternity" or not will be left for the Masonic brethren to decide. His estate comprised the whole of the present village of Stony Brook north of the brook, extending to the bounds of Duxbury, besides tracts of land in other parts of the town. All that portion first mentioned was bequeathed to his four younger sons, viz: Israel, Ephraim, David, and Hezekiah. Many interesting facts could be recounted relating to this distinguished man, whom Kingston should never forget to honor, but the limited time forbids. He died Feb. 20, 1704, and was buried by the side of his father on the ancient burial hill at Plymouth. His gravestone bears the following inscription:—

Here lyes the Body

OF THE

HONOURABLE MAJOR WILLIAM BRADFORD,

WHO

EXPIRED FEBRUARY Yᵉ 20th, 1703-4.

AGED 79 YEARS.

He lived long but still was doing good
And in his country's service lost much blood.
After a life well spent he's now at rest,
His very name and memory is blest.

Joseph Bradford, the youngest son of the governor, lived half a mile from the mouth of Jones River at a place called Flat House Dock. He died in 1715. Major John Bradford, the eldest son of Major William, lived in the house still in existence near the railroad at the Landing. This house was partially burned by the Indians during Philip's War. The circumstances connected with this event may be interesting to the younger people. The story is this: Major Bradford had removed to the guard-house (which may have been the ancient Cobb house, as there is a tradition that it was formerly a garrison or fort), and was returning in company with others to take some goods away when he discovered his house to be on fire, and saw an

VICINITY OF JONES RIVER,

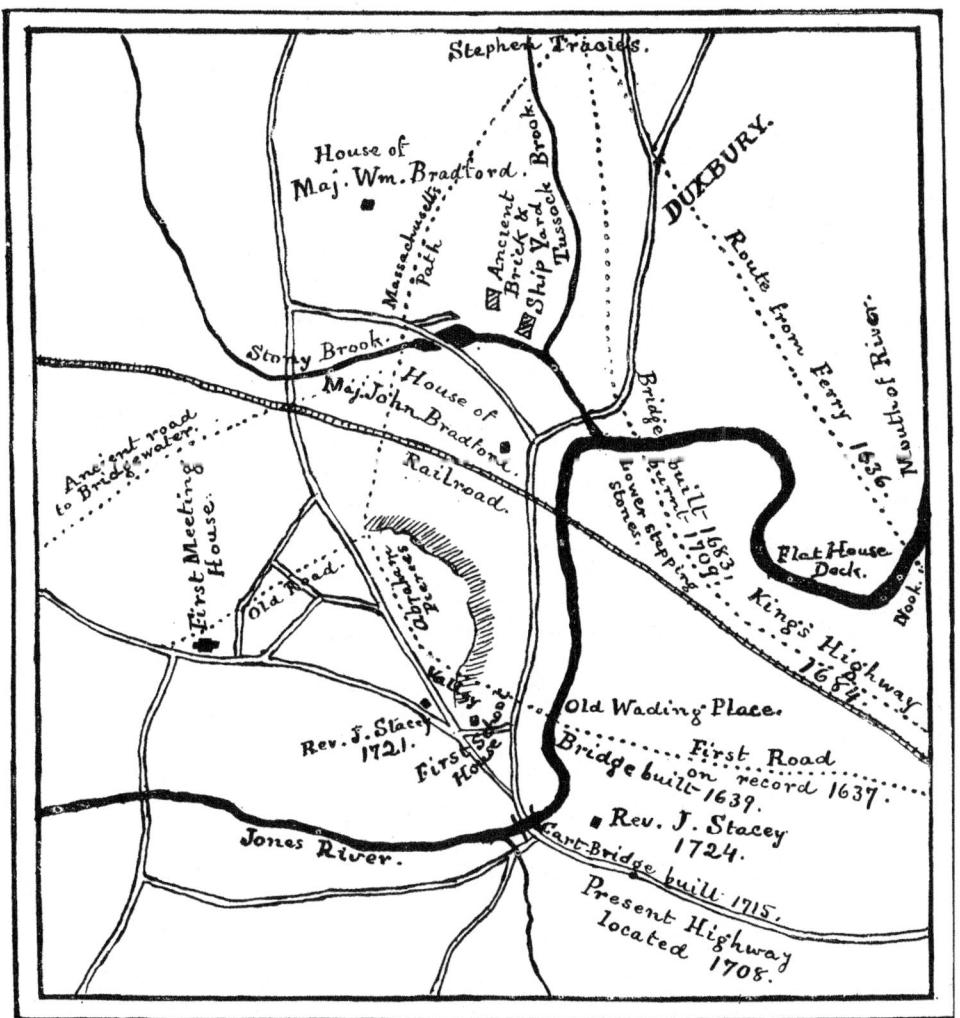

Three Routes from Plymouth to Stephen Tracie's in the 17th Century and some of the localities noticed in the Historical Sketch.

From O. C. Records May 10, 1637. "It is agreed that the heighways both for horse and cart shall be as followeth. From the town of Plymouth to Jones River as it was cleared, provided it be holpen at Mr. Allerton's by going through the old cowe yard at the river, the place being commonly called the Old Wading Place and so through a valley up the hill and then to turn straight to Abraham Pierce's ground and through his ground as it is now marked and so the old path to Massachusetts leaving Mr. Bradford's house upon the west, and from Mr. Bradford's house to Steephen Tracey's ground as the way now lyeth, being already trenched a foote way from the lower stepping stones to Steephen Tracie's the heighway lying through Steephen Tracie's feild now enclosed. Also we allow a way from Francis Billington's gronnd through the nooke as it now lyeth to the ferry and from the ferry to Steephen Tracie's house and so through the meadow to the bridg."

Indian on the brow of Abram's Hill, waving his blanket and shouting to his comrades that the white men were coming. They fled into a dense swamp by the frog-pond at the base of the hill, and were pursued by the major, who fired at them, killing one as he supposed by seeing him fall, but on reaching the spot was surprised at not finding the body. As it happened, the Indian was only severely wounded, and was able immediately to crawl behind a log of fallen wood, and thus escaped notice. After the war was over the affair was explained to Bradford by the Indian, and the marks of the wound in his side were shown. Major Bradford held many offices, being a deputy and representative to the General Court on several occasions. He was the principal founder of the new town, and a promoter of its interests by gifts of land for public purposes.

Caleb Cook, who will be remembered in connection with the death of King Philip, lived at Rocky Nook. He was a soldier and was placed with an Indian by Col. Church to watch, and if possible, kill Philip. When the chance came, Cook snapped his gun, but it missed fire. He then bade the Indian fire, and the mighty chieftain was instantly killed. The Indian gave up his gun to Cook, and it was kept in the family for several generations. Part of it is now in Pilgrim Hall as a relic.

Edward Gray, the most prosperous merchant in the colony at the time of his death in 1681, lived in Rocky Nook on the same estate where some of his descendants still dwell.

William Paddy and Thomas Willet, merchants, bought a house at Jones River in 1648 belonging to Edmond Freeman, of Sandwich. Mr. Willet traded with the Dutch at New York, and became so accustomed to them, their language, etc., that after the surrender of the place to the English, he rendered the Commissioners of Appeals great service, and became so popular that he was elected the first English mayor of New York. He died in Swansey in 1674.

Thomas Prence, the governor of Plymouth Colony seventeen years, at one time owned the farm that first belonged to Mr. Allerton and afterwards to Elder Cushman.

Charles Chauncy, the minister of Plymouth and Scituate, and finally President of Harvard College, had a grant of ten acres of land at the North Meadow by the river in 1640.

The names of Armstrong, Bartlett, Brown, Combe, Crowe, Curtis, Cole, Doane, Lee, Wright, Winter, and others appear upon the records as land owners in this vicinity. Thus an attempt has been made to notice all the principal persons who took up lands or resided in this part of the colony, and it is pleasing to know that so many of the distinguished founders once inhabited the soil of Kingston, and that the events connected with their lives can thus be perpetuated in the memory of their posterity, and others who may from time to time occupy those same lands once trodden by the Pilgrims. May future generations forever cherish the names of those "ancient worthies" who first planted the seeds of civilization on these Western shores and bequeathed to us so many blessings!

HIGHWAYS.

For an unknown period previous to the settlement of the colonies by the English the country had been inhabited by tribes of Indians, who had their paths or trails connecting different points and the more distant regions one with another. Those paths in many cases were doubtless used by our forefathers in passing from place to place, and finally became established roads. In the early records the "path to the Massachusetts" or the "Massachusetts path" (which connected this part of the colony with that in the vicinity of Boston) is often mentioned.

It probably crossed Jones River near the almshouse, and then up Abram's Hill, through the valley just north of the house of the late Wiswall S. Stetson, and thence in a northeasterly direction towards the present estate of Samuel Loring, Esq., of Duxbury. The first bridge over Jones River was built in 1639, near the place just mentioned, and in a few years afterwards another one was built farther down the river near the fish wharf. As early as 1636 there was a ferry established nearly at the mouth of the river, and Joseph Rogers was allowed a penny for the transportation of each person. In 1684 the King's highway was laid out, and after passing from Plymouth through Rocky Nook, crossed the river at the lower bridge. In 1707 the town voted "that it is a great burden and charge to maintain two bridges over Jones River when one might answer, and that application be made to the County Court and the Court of Barnstable that a bridge might be built higher up the river." The next year, 1708, the highway was changed to its present location, and the first cart-bridge was built there in 1715 at a cost of £80. About the time this new road was opened, the old lower bridge was burned, as was supposed by an incendiary. While the officers of the law were endeavoring to detect the person, a wag reported to them that he saw a man going to the bridge with a live coal in his hand, but on being pressed for further information, at last told them it was only a certain gentleman walking hand in hand with a young lady whose name was Cole. The other old bridge near by the new road was ordered by the court to be taken down, as it was dangerous for travel.

In the early times there was a road from Stony Brook, running towards Bridgewater across the corner of Evergreen Cemetery, following nearly the footpath that still exists. There was also a highway across the old burying-ground, from where the Town Hall is now located, to a point near the house of Mr. Lewis Ripley, thus separating the old church from the graveyard. Any one can now notice that the old gravestones, say previous to 1760, are to be found at the northwest part of the old ground. The road from the church to the Patuxet House was not laid out until 1759.

JONES RIVER PARISH, INCORPORATION OF KINGSTON, ETC.

At the beginning of the last century, or soon after the year 1700, the inhabitants in the region of Jones River had so increased that they numbered more than forty families, and they began to feel the necessity of a withdrawal from the old town, but there was no action in the matter until March, 1717, when a request was made to the town for a separation. This was refused, and shortly after a petition signed by forty-one persons was directed to "His Excellency, Samuel Shute, Esq., Captain General and Governor-in-Chief, in and over His Majesty's Province of the Massachusetts Bay, etc. The Council and Representatives in General Court assembled," in which they set forth the difficulties they labored under by living so far from the meeting-house, many residing at a distance of six or seven miles, and the most of them above four miles, etc., etc. After a full hearing upon the question, the General Court passed an Act in November, 1717, setting off the north part of Plymouth with a small portion of Plympton and Pembroke, as a precinct or parish. As the Act provided that they should suitably maintain a minister, the people of the new parish soon began to make preparations to build the meeting-house, and a call was given to Mr. Thomas Paine to be their minister, but he was not settled, and nothing more is recorded concerning the ministry until we find that "Mr. Joseph Stacie began to preach July 26, 1720." On the 5th of January, 1721, Major

John Bradford deeded a lot of land to the minister, on which was soon erected the parsonage house. Mr. Stacey sold this house to Thomas Croade in 1724, and afterwards lived in the house that formerly stood near the large elm-tree on the grounds of Joseph A. Holmes, and which was not taken down until about 1843.

Only a little more than seven years had elapsed after the incorporation of Jones River parish when a serious trouble arose concerning the schools. As early as 1696 it was voted by the town that the school-master for the fourth quarter should "*remove no farther southward in said towne for settlement to keepe scool than John Gray's.*" In 1714 £20 was allowed to the north end of the town "*to build a scool house somewhare neere Jacob Cook's,*" and the same year Major John Bradford gave a lot of land for it to be built upon near the corner, just westerly from the house of the late Capt. James Sever. A school-house which stood on the same land is well remembered by many persons, as it was not removed until 1826, just fifty years ago. At a very excited meeting Feb. 15, 1725, it was voted to have but one school in the town. As the inhabitants in the north parish had enjoyed for several years a separate school, this action of the town greatly exasperated them, and to compromise the matter somewhat, it was voted at the next meeting to allow them what they were annually rated or taxed for the school, and no more, towards maintaining one among themselves. The result of this meeting seemed to determine the future action of the people of Jones River parish, for the same month they voted at a precinct meeting "*to petition y Great and General Court to become a township.*" During that year the matter was urged and opposed by the different parties, as a majority of the people of the town of Plymouth were strongly against the separation; but on the third day of

June, 1726, the bounds of the intended new town were decided upon, and on the 16th day O. S., corresponding to the 27th N. S., the following Act passed:—

ANNO REGNI REGIS GEORGII DUODECIMO.

AN ACT

Passed by the Great and General Court or Assembly of His Majesty's Province of the Massachusetts Bay for Dividing the Town of Plymouth, and erecting a New Town there by the name of Kingston.

Whereas the town of Plymouth within the county of Plymouth is of great extent for length and lyes commodiously for Two Townships and the North Precinct thereof being of late sufficiently filled with Inhabitants who labour under great Difficulties on several accounts and have there upon addressed this Court that they may be set off a distinct and separate Township; Be it therefore Enacted by the Lieut. Governor, Council and Representatives in General Court assembled and by the authority of the same; That all the Lands lying within the said North Precinct in Plymouth aforesaid, particularly described and bounded by an Order of this Court passed at their present Session, be and hereby are set off and constituted a separate Township by the name of Kingston; And that the Inhabitants of said Township be vested with the Powers, Privileges and Immunities that the Inhabitants of any Town of this Province, by Law are or ought to be vested with. Provided, and be it further enacted; That nothing in this act contained, shall be construed, deemed, judged or intended to hinder or prejudice the right and interest of all or any persons whatsoever in any of the Common and Undivided Lands within the Towns of Plymouth and Kingston aforesaid, but the same shall remain as heretofore. Provided also, and be it further Enacted, That the Inhabitants of the said Town of Kingston shall be liable and subject (notwithstanding their being set off and constituted a Township aforesaid) to pay their proportion of all Province, County and Town rates for this present year in the Towns to which they respectively belonged, and shall be accordingly assessed in such Towns in the same manner as they would have been if this Act had never been made; Anything before contained to the contrary notwithstanding.

Passed in Council and signed,

J. WILLARD, *Sec'y.*

Passed in the House of Representatives and signed,

WM. DUDLEY, *Spk'r.*

Consented to,
WM. DUMMER.

It is said that Lieut.-Gov. Dummer suggested the name of the new town on the 28th of May, that being the birthday of His Majesty King George the First, then the reigning sovereign of England.

By order of the General Court Major Bradford issued on the 13th of August the first warrant for a town meeting, to be held on the 29th of the same month, and at that meeting the following officers were chosen; Major John Bradford, Moderator; Joseph Mitchell, Clerk; Benj. Eaton, Thomas Croad, and Jacob Mitchell, Selectmen and Assessors; Ensign Wrestling Brewster, Treasurer; Joseph Mitchell, Constable; Seth Chipman, Tithing Man; John Gray and Samuel Foster, Hog Reeves; Robert Cook and Jacob Cook Jr., Fence Viewers; Samuel Ring, Surveyor.

ANNALS OF THE TOWN.

Having passed the period of the incorporation of Kingston, I must necessarily pass rapidly over the next fifty years, simply noting a few facts or events. In 1730 the name of Giles Rickard, the school-master, first appears upon the records, though he had probably been employed previously. In 1740 Capt. Gershom Bradford was sent as the first representative to the General Court. Previous to this, the town had sent excuses for not sending. Rev. Joseph Stacey died Aug. 25, 1741, after a ministry of twenty-one years. Rev. Thaddeus Maccarty was the next settled minister, being ordained in November, 1742. In 1743 a reward of ten pounds was offered to any one who should kill a wolf within the limits of the town, and the following year it is recorded that a wolf was killed. In 1745, during Rev. George Whitefield's career in this vicinity a trouble arose with the minister, Mr. Maccarty. The town voted " not to allow itinerant preachers to preach in the meeting house," and "that hooks and staples be put to the casements that nobody may get in at unseasonable hours to do damage in ye meeting house, etc., etc." Mr. Maccarty was displeased and asked for his dismission, which was readily granted in November, 1745. It is said that both minister and people afterwards regretted the action taken at that time.

The third minister was Rev. William Rand, who was settled in 1746. He had previously been settled at Sunderland, and his opinion in regard to Mr. Whitefield was just the opposite of Mr. Maccarty's.

Joseph Mitchell, who had held the office of clerk since the incorporation of the town with the exception of two years, died 1754. It was voted in 1756, "that the town stores of powder, balls, &c., be lodged in the garret of the meeting-house." Until 1764 the meeting-house had no steeple, and that year one was built and the first bell of the town was placed in it. This year died Nicholas Sever, Esq., aged eighty-four years. He was the first of the once prominent family of that name in Kingston, and now but one of his descendants resides in the town. He graduated at Harvard College, 1701, was ordained minister at Dover, N. H., 1711, and dismissed 1715. After being a tutor in Harvard College, he settled in Kingston about 1728, and was, for a number years, a judge of one of the Plymouth County Courts. After the disturbances at Boston, caused by the Stamp Act of 1766, a meeting was called to see if the town would vote for compensation to the sufferers by the riotous proceedings, and a majority was against it.

Deacon Wrestling Brewster, the first town treasurer, who continued in that office until 1751, died Jan. 1, 1767, in his seventy-third year. He was of the third generation in descent from the Elder, and was born in Duxbury, removing to Kingston previous to 1720, as about that time he built the house belonging to the estate of the late Elisha Brewster. Oct. 14, 1771, it was voted "to allow Benj. Cook the sum of eight shillings for a coffin and liquor at the funeral of James Howland." Although this person was one of the town's poor, yet, according to the custom of those days, all proper respect was shown him.

REVOLUTIONARY HISTORY.

On the 12th of January, 1773, a meeting was called to consider a pamphlet published by order of the town of Boston, in which many infringements of the rights of the inhabitants were pointed out, etc. On the 4th of February, the town addressed the following answer to the Committee of Correspondence, of Boston : —

Gentlemen: — The town having duly considered the same, are clearly of the opinion that they are fully entitled to all those rights as by you stated, and that any attempt to deprive us of them is an infringement of our just rights. It gives us the greatest concern to see that, notwithstanding the immense advantages accruing to Great Britain from her trade with the colonies, advantages vastly exceeding the expenses incurred for their protection, that the Parliament of Great Britain should adopt a system with regard to the colonies which effectually divests them of their rights as Englishmen and subjects, and reduces them to a condition little better than that of slaves, — a system which, if adhered to, will, we fear eventually terminate in their own ruin. But notwithstanding such has been the unremitted, unvaried plan of administration towards the colonies for years past, we cannot but hope a due regard for their own safety and real interest will at length induce them to redress the grievances we so justly complain of. We shall always be ready to co-operate with our brethren in any legal and constitutional measures tending thereto. Slavery is ever preceded by sleep: May the colonists be ever watchful over their just rights, and may their liberties be fixed on such a basis as that they may be transmitted inviolate to the latest posterity.

Sept. 26, 1774, a meeting of the towns of Plymouth County, by their committees or delegates, was held at the tavern of Widow Loring, in Plympton, and John Thomas, Esq., Capt. John Gray, and William Drew were the Kingston delegates. Subsequently, these same gentlemen, with Hon. William Sever,

Deacon Ebenezer Washburn, Mr. Benjamin Cook, Mr. Peleg Wadsworth, Jedediah Holmes, and Capt. Joseph Bartlett were chosen the Committee of Correspondence. The minute company was probably formed in 1774, as in the early part of 1775 the town voted "to purchase thirty-three stand of good fire-arms, with all accoutrements suitable to equip thirty-three soldiers." This company was commanded by Capt. Peleg Wadsworth; Seth Drew was lieutenant, and Joseph Sampson, ensign. As soon as the news of the Lexington battle reached the Old Colony, the Kingston company marched with Col. Cotton's regiment to attack Balfour's regiment of British troops, which was stationed at Marshfield. After arriving there, a conference of officers was held, and Capt. Wadsworth, being dissatisfied with the delay, marched his company to within a short distance of the enemy; but his numbers were too small to venture an attack, and before any action took place, Balfour conveyed his troops through the Cut River, and when on board the sloops, which were anchored off Brant Rock, sailed for Boston. Thus the Kingston minute company has its place in history.

Of the officers in the Revolutionary army, the most prominent ones who went from Kingston were Gen. Peleg Wadsworth (a native of Duxbury, but for several years a resident of Kingston), Gen. Jno. Thomas, and Major Seth Drew. Gen. Wadsworth distinguished himself by many acts during the war, and finally lived and died in Maine in 1829. Of the eminent services of Gen. Thomas I need not speak, as they are so well known to all who are acquainted with the early history of the army at Roxbury and Dorchester Heights, and as such honorable mention has been made of them by the orator on this occasion. Major Drew was in the army throughout the whole war, being at Saratoga when Burgoyne surrendered, also at Trenton,

Monmouth, and in the vicinity of West Point during that memorable campaign. He was one of the court-martial appointed to try Joshua Hett Smith, accused of being an accomplice of Major André.

Simeon Sampson, the distinguished naval commander, was a native of Kingston. He was appointed by the Provincial Congress of Massachusetts the first naval captain in the service, and commanded the brig "Independence," and afterwards the "Mars," both vessels being built at the Kingston Landing. While in the first-named vessel in 1776 he captured five prizes, but was himself soon after taken by Capt. Dawson, after a bloody conflict. March 24, 1777, Samuel Foster, Charles Foster, and Wrestling Brewster were considered internal enemies of the government. The Messrs. Foster were tried by a court in the meeting-house, and both were sent on board a guard-ship in Boston Harbor, where they remained ten months. At this time several persons left town, as they were attached to the royal cause, and it was made very uncomfortable for any one suspected of being a Tory, as he was in constant danger of a coat of tar and feathers by the vigilance committee, to say nothing of the numerous indignities they at times received. At one time, while the British soldiers were stationed in Marshfield, a man by the name of Dunbar carried an ox, which had been slaughtered by a Tory of that town, to Plymouth for the purpose of selling it. As soon as the facts were discovered the vigilance committee took the case in hand. Dunbar was put inside of the carcass with the tripe tied around his neck, and in that condition was sent to the committee at Kingston. On arriving at the liberty pole here, the contents of the cart were tipped out, and after a sort of demonstration was made, the cart was reloaded and sent to the authorities of Duxbury, where Dunbar was subjected to the same treatment he had previously received in this town. He was then taken to the bounds of Marshfield and there left, his escort not caring to risk a contact with the troops stationed there.

Another incident of those times of a different nature will be mentioned in this connection. A certain sea captain, whose sympathies were decidedly with the Royalists, had absented himself from public worship for a long time on account of the revolutionary proclivities of Parson Rand. But it came to his ears that on a certain Sunday the minister would read a proclamation from the king. This so delighted him that he resolved to attend divine service on that day, and Mr. Rand did read the king's proclamation; but to the great consternation of the Tory, the minister turned over the document, on the back of which he had written his sermon, containing many severe allusions to King George and his advisers in Parliament, and it proved to be a sermon more decided in its political nature than Mr. Rand had ever before preached. He listened to it until he became very angry, then left the house in an excited manner, slamming the pew-door after him and shuffling his feet on the floor as he passed down the aisle. To irritate him a little more, just as he was passing out of the house a member of the congregation cried out to him, "*Shet the door arter ye, Captain!*" much to the amusement of the audience.

At a meeting in 1778, William Drew and Nicholas Davis, Jr., were chosen "to purchase articles of clothing, etc., to be sent to the suffering soldiers in the army." On the 14th of March, 1779, the Rev. William Rand, after a faithful ministry of thirty-three years, died suddenly of apoplexy, aged seventy-nine years. In July of the same year Wm. Drew, Esq., was chosen a delegate to attend the convention at Cambridge for framing a new State Constitution. May 22, 1780, the town voted " to concur with the church in giving Mr. Willis a call to the work of the Gospel ministry in this town," his salary to be £80, to be paid partly in Indian corn, rye, pork, beef, etc., at specified prices. A settlement of about £133 was also granted him. He was ordained Oct. 18 of the same year, and continued in the ministry forty-eight years, until he resigned in 1828. He lived until March 6, 1847, when he died in the ninety-first year of his age. The first election of State officers under the new Massachusetts Constitution took place Sept. 4, 1780, and the Kingston vote for governor was, for Hon. John Hancock, 13, for Hon. James Bowdoin, 12. About this time the paper currency had become so greatly depreciated that no confidence could be placed in its value, for in December $75 per bushel was allowed the soldiers for the corn that was due them, and in May, 1781, it was voted " to allow Mr. John Fuller's account for £22 10s. old currency, *one hard dollar*. The ancient burial ground, that was given to the town for a burying place by Major John Bradford in 1721, remained without an enclosure for sixty-six years, when in 1787 a wall was built to protect it. There the remains of most of the founders of the town, with their descendants, in some cases to the number of seven or eight generations, repose, and there, also, rest three of the four earlier ministers (Messrs. Stacey, Rand, and Willis), whose pastorates, with the exception of Mr. Maccarty's three years, extended over a space of about one hundred and eight years. The earliest inscription there bears the date of Feb. 14, 1718, and down to the year 1860 nine hundred and thirty-five names were inscribed on the gravestones in that old burial place. As many graves have no monument or stone to mark them, the whole number buried there can only be imagined. Down to the year 1840 this continued to be the only public burying place, but about that time the old ground was enlarged on the northerly side, and since 1854 the beautiful

Evergreen Cemetery has been connected with this latter portion, so that the ancient resting-place of our fathers, with that of the present generation, are still in one enclosure The Hon. William Sever, Esq., was chosen a delegate to the State Convention for ratifying the United States Constitution, which was held in January, 1788.

The most remarkable case of longevity in this vicinity was that of Ebenezer Cobb. On the first day of April, 1794, he completed his hundredth year and continued to live until December, 1801, when in his one hundred and eighth year. Being born in 1694, he lived in the seventeenth, eighteenth, and nineteenth centuries. As he was five years old before Mary Allerton, the last of the Pilgrims, died, it makes him the link that connects the Mayflower Pilgrims with the present time, for aged people are now living who recollect of seeing this centenarian; and it is a peculiar pleasure that we have two of that number on the platform here to-day, the venerable Rev. Job Washburn, of Rockport, Me., now in his ninetieth year, who is visiting his native town probably for the last time, on this interesting occasion, and the Hon. Joseph R. Chandler, a distinguished son of Kingston, now a resident of Philadelphia.

The first meeting-house, that had stood for eighty years, was demolished in 1798, and a new one was built that year, which is well remembered by many of us, as it was not taken down until May, 1851, after standing fifty-three years. The present church edifice of the First Congregational Society occupies the same site as the two which preceded it, and some of the timber from the very first building was used in the construction of the last.

I did intend before finishing this sketch to notice many things which must be passed over. A mere reference to the schools of seventy years ago will doubtless cause many of the aged people of this community to think of their youthful days, when they were instructed by Mr. Martin Parris as he went from one section of the town to the other, and thus in his circuit was teacher of the whole.

A very important business carried on in town in the ancient times and down to within a few years was that of ship building. Vessels were built on Jones River or Stony Brook before 1714. The Stetsons and Drews were builders at a very early date, and the latter family can count back at least six generations who were engaged in the same business.

During the first sixty years of the present century Joseph Holmes built seventy-five or more vessels, while in the same period many others were launched from the yards of the Drews, Bartletts, and Delanos.

CONCLUSION.

Two hundred and fifty-five years have passed since the first settlement of New England at Plymouth, and I have endeavored in this imperfect sketch to notice the interesting facts and speak of the most important events that transpired in the vicinity of Jones River for one hundred and seventy-five years of that period. As Kingston has shown so good a record in the years gone by, may we, her children, assembled here to-day, forever honor the old town from whence we sprung, and keep alive the memories of the worthy deeds of our ancestors, so that our children and their descendants may never forget the starting-point of their race, in this good Old Colony town.

AFTER DINNER SPEECHES.

1. The day we celebrate, designated for the public recital of our town history by the Proclamation of Divine Providence.

SPEECH OF HON. GEORGE B. LORING, OF SALEM.

Ladies and Gentlemen, — After the exhaustive and elaborate addresses to which we have listened to-day, it would seem as if there were no more to be said with regard to the events which you have met to commemorate. But I have felt that I should not do justice to my own natural feelings were I to fail in attempting, at least, to perform the part which has been assigned me. This spot is filled with personal interest to my mind. The hero and heroine of this locality, and of that period in history out of which grew the organization of this town, stand at the head of one branch of my own family, and bind me with a strong and tender bond to the people who made these shores immortal. I have always taken especial delight in the personal contest between Miles Standish and John Alden, feeling that the very beginning of my fortune and fate, ay, of life itself was fixed when the valiant captain surrendered at the feet of the fair Priscilla Mullins, and John Alden, a successful and triumphant suitor, laid the foundation of that family from which my paternal grandmother sprang, and whose name she bore. The landscape here is the setting to my mind of a picture which I never grow weary in contemplating. I cannot forget, moreover, that there is an unadjusted account of charity and kindness still open between the colony at Plymouth and the colony at Naumkeag, which I now represent, an account created when the Pilgrims sent their wise and learned physician to heal the distemper which broke out among the followers of John Endicott, and threatened to destroy them. Perhaps I, as a quasi-physician from old Essex, can, on this occasion and at this late day, perform some service here which may be considered a humble and inadequate offset to the debt incurred by my ancestors.

But more than all this, the town itself in which we have assembled stands in history, to my mind, as a representative spot. The planting of colonies in various ages of the world constitutes one of the most interesting chapters which man is called upon to contemplate. The power of a great nationality manifests itself as much in the quality of the colonies it sends forth as in any more conspicuous step in its career. The swarms which poured forth from Greece and Rome to occupy the remote regions of the globe in those early days, told of the vital force of these great nationalities, and gave them an influence not surpassed by that acquired by their schools and their social and civil organization. It was the principles which the colonies bore with them that indicated the character of the parent stock. Imagine then, if you can, the significance of a colony whose fountain sprang from the foot of Plymouth Rock. When your ancestors started forth from the immortal colony which settled there, they bore with them the very foundation of our government itself. They carried with them as the ark of their covenant those doctrines of state and society which have enabled our country to endure, and have given a grand significance to this centennial anniversary of our nation's birth. The people who inherited the character of John Carver, the immortal governor, and the philosophy and example of Winslow and Bradford and Brewster have a right to a high distinction, unknown to many a more conspicuous and imposing nationality. For let it be remembered that the associations which cluster here to-day belong to the immortal events of history,— events which will not be forgotten when the glory of many a conquest shall have faded from the memory of man.

I always contemplate with great pride and satisfaction the work performed by our fathers here, simple and unpretending as it was. The historian of this occasion has told us that in the early days of the colonies, a path was cut through the forest having Plymouth at one end and Boston at the other. Along this rude highway the defiant colonists of Plymouth and Massachusetts Bay are said to have travelled in those heroic times, when the solemnity of the primeval forests was a fitting retreat for the serious and determined adventurers, who brought with them from the Old World all the great doctrines of freedom and right upon which to found the New. It was along this path that the advocates of those principles of church and state, which we now enjoy passed along on their sacred errand. Here might have been heard the truth which was thundered from the gallery of the Old South and echoed through Faneuil Hall in the days of Adams and Otis and Warren and Quincy, the orators of the uprising people. Here might have been heard those doctrines which were woven into the Declaration of Independence. Here was laid the foundation of universal freedom, and that human law out of which grew the Proclamation of Emancipation. Here was written the sacred word borne by our soldiers on the point of their bayonets through the great civil war, and here, on this path, in those primeval days, might have been found the prophets of American nationality. It is on this path, my friends, that the American people are travelling to-day.

Allow me, then, to propose to you: "The Massachusetts path, — may it encircle this continent, and become the highway along which a great people may travel to never-ending glory and renown."

---

2. Kingston, though born under a monarchy and of royal name, has ever been a most loyal portion of the Great Republic.

RESPONSE OF HON. E. S. TOBEY, Post-Master of Boston.

Mr. President, Ladies and Gentlemen, — I confess to a degree of sympathy for you that, after the eloquent words of the distinguished gentleman who has just preceded me, you are obliged to listen to the common-place remarks of the speaker. I am not unmindful that it is the accident of birth, rather than any special merit of mine, which has placed me in so prominent relations to this truly interesting and commemorative occasion. As it is a kind of family gathering, I may, perhaps, be permitted the liberty of referring to some early local reminiscences, even though they be personal. This is not the first time that a topic has been assigned to me by my fellow-townsmen.

Memory at once recalls to my mind and, perhaps, also to the minds of some early friends whom I now have the pleasure of addressing, the fact that, at the age of ten years, when a scholar in the academy, the well-known soliloquy of Alexander Selkirk was given me on which to exercise my powers of declamation, in those familiar lines commencing, —

> "I am monarch of all I survey,
> My right there is none to dispute."

I can assure you that these early and delusive ideas of universal empire have long since been dispelled, and my rights, although in my judgment often remarkably well-founded, have been successfully disputed. But deeply as this and other incidents of my early school-days are graven on my memory, not less vivid are the recollections of the old church, with its peculiar but dignified architecture, and its equally dignified pastor, who ministered at its altar for so long a period.

The tones of its bell, as in solemn cadence it noted the departure of a beloved friend or neighbor, seem still to echo in my ears, reviving the memory of the honored dead; and although no "storied urn or ambitious monument" marks their final resting-place, the record of their worthy deeds and private virtues will ever be enshrined in the hearts of their descendants.

But no longer to indulge in these reminiscences I turn to the sentiment to which I have been invited to respond. No one can question the fact that our worthy progenitors had no love for monarchy in any form. It is, however, evident that they did not wholly lose their taste for royalty, or at least for some of its more pleasing associations, as partially indicated by their adoption for our native town the name applied by the Duke of Kingston to his extensive domain in England.

As to the loyalty of Kingston to the Great Republic we need no further evidence than is contained in the interesting sketch given us by the faithful historian of this occasion as to the services of our fellow-townsmen in the war of the Revolution, the maritime war of 1812, and in the recent war of the Rebellion. But evidence of loyalty and patriotism is not confined to either military or naval service. "If War has its victories, Peace has its victories too." Kingston has shown her loyalty to the principles of Republican government by her full share of influence in shaping both state and national legislation. Although never directly represented in the halls of Congress, she has had representatives there in her sons, who have been readily

* Rev. Mr. Willis.

adopted by the States to which they had transferred their residence. Our venerable friend * who honors us with his presence to-day, was, as you are aware, a representative in Congress from Pennsylvania, and was subsequently appointed by the President of the United States as Minister to Naples. The late Hon. John Holmes was also adopted by Maine, and ably represented her in the United States Senate. The sons of Kingston who have removed to other parts of the State have also been chosen to participate in determining her political policy.

And, now, friends, aside from the social and intellectual enjoyments of this pleasant occasion, what is its practical lesson? Is it not that it may deepen our convictions of duty, and inspire us, each and every one, with an earnest and sincere desire so to discharge our responsibilities, that those who shall at some distant period gather here may be able to testify to our fidelity to the principles and virtues transmitted to us by the fathers whose memory to-day we seek to revive and perpetuate?

---

3. The Commonwealth of Massachusetts, all the more flourishing and fruitful because engrafted upon Pilgrim stock and watered by Pilgrim springs.

RESPONDED TO BY HON. HENRY B. PEIRCE, SECRETARY OF STATE.

His Excellency, Gov. Rice was expected to speak to this sentiment but was unexpectedly detained by " an official duty." The Secretary, after explaining the enforced absence of the Governor and apologizing for him, in a short but unreportable speech put the audience into the best possible good humor by his wit and drollery, which served greatly to mitigate the keen disappointment felt by all.

It is proper to add that the Governor's Private Secretary and personal Staff were present and participated in the festivities of the day.

* Hon. Joseph R. Chandler, of Philadelphia.

4. Plymouth: Our Mother Town. We invite her to join us to-day in welcoming her grandchildren to this feast.

SPEECH OF HON. WILLIAM T. DAVIS, OF PLYMOUTH.

Mr. President, — In riding from Plymouth into your village this morning, had I not on various occasions in an official capacity been called upon to define the boundary between the two towns I should have found it difficult to determine where Plymouth ended and Kingston began. The population is so continuous from one town to the other that I am not sure a scheme of annexation will not soon be contemplated. Whether Kingston shall be annexed to Plymouth or Plymouth to Kingston will be a question in which your taxpayers will have far more interest than ours. It has already been suggested that Plymouth might supply Kingston with water, but I am inclined to think that the suggestion has its origin in the fact that the other ingredient of your half and half she supplies you with too bountifully already. Of Plymouth gas you will probably have no need, as I fear that the specimen exhibited here to-day will be more than you desire of that article.

But seriously, sir, I thank you for the privilege of being here to-day, and in behalf of the town of Plymouth which I unworthily represent, of tendering to you the congratulations of a parent to her child on the one hundred and fiftieth anniversary of its birth. On this interesting occasion Plymouth mingles her rejoicings with yours and repeats your cordial welcome to the sons and daughters of Kingston gathered around this board. I cannot fail to remember that for more than a century after the settlement of that ancient town you were bone of her bone and flesh of her flesh, that your history and hers were identical, and that now the same ancestral glories which stir her pride, kindle also a warmer glow in the blood which courses through your veins. Your early traditions and hers are the same; the sacred places where our fathers lived and died are scattered over your domain; the names of Adams, Bradford, Cooke, Cushman, Fuller, Gray, Holmes and others in your midst attest your Pilgrim descent; and yonder river, which in 1620 bore the shallop of the Mayflower on its bosom, still winds its reluctant way to the sea as if loving to linger among your homes and repeat its story of those early days. But, sir, these are not the associations which the voices of the hour recall. More recent memories cluster around the day you celebrate, — memories exclusively your own, which no stranger can either appropriate or share. The history, however, of your town, from the organization of the north parish of Plymouth in 1717, and the incorporation of your municipality in 1726, has been so thoroughly and accurately portrayed that nothing is left to be culled by those whose fortune it is to follow your orator and historian. Its current has flowed on with placid stream through lengthened periods of ordinary municipal life, marked only by the intelligence, enterprise, and thrift of its people, and through shorter and more eventful seasons of revolutionary and rebellious wars, in which its patriotism and courage have been tested and proved.

But I cannot forget that to a Kingston man belongs the honor of having received the first naval commission in the war of our independence and that the vessel in which he sailed and fought was the first vessel placed in commission by the Provincial Congress and was built on the banks and launched into the waters of your river. I hold in my hand the sword of that gallant hero, Simeon Sampson, the sword which he wore in one of the most bloody naval battles of the war, and which his captor,

Capt. Dawson returned to him in recognition of his heroism and courage.

Nor must I fail to pay due respect to the memory of him to whom no more than justice has been done to-day, one of those immortal men with whom Washington " went shoulder to shoulder into the Revolution, and on whom his great arm leaned for support." A physician of education and repute, a commander of provincial troops under Gen. John Winslow in the war of 1756, a delegate to the convention of Plymouth County in 1774, a member of the Provincial Congress in that and the following year, lieutenant-general in the provincial army, and brigadier-general in the continental army, Gen. John Thomas was selected to command the expedition against Canada in 1776, in which he lost his life. To have produced such a man, active yet judicious, resolute yet prudent, fearless yet sagacious, high-bred yet beyond ordinary measure kind to his men and thoughtful of their comfort and health, trusted and beloved by Washington and pronounced by the inexorable pen of Bancroft to have been the best general officer in the colony, Kingston, on this her day of jubilee, may well be proud.

Nor must I hesitate to correct the modest claim of your historian, that Kingston furnished sixty-one men for the war of the Revolution. I have brought from my library a contemporaneous official record of the men raised by the various towns in Plymouth County during that memorable struggle, and I find in the manuscript which I hold in my hand the names of one hundred men whose enlistments attest your active patriotism. I also hold in my hand the original census of Plymouth county taken soon after the war, containing the names of heads of families and the number in each family, and showing the population of Kingston to have been nine hundred and ninety-nine. Thus the record shows that from ten to twelve per cent of the whole population and nearly one half of the adult male citizens of the town took active part in the service of their country. If there are other towns in the commonwealth which can show a better revolutionary record, I challenge them here and now to produce it.

Of the part which Kingston performed in the recent war of the Rebellion, I do not propose to speak. I assure you, however, I know it well, for no one had a better opportunity than myself of observing the patriotic liberality which characterized its citizens and the eminent ability with which its municipal affairs were conducted in meeting with full measure the requirements of the war.

In thus alluding, sir, to the pages in the history of your town on which the record of its patriotic deeds may be found, and which I trust are closed forever, let me in closing express the hope that hereafter neither wars nor rumors of wars may disturb your people, but that for all coming time, peace, prosperity, and happiness may reign within your borders.

---

5. The Legends of Kingston.

SPEECH OF HON. JOSEPH R. CHANDLER.

Mr. President, — The gentleman who preceded me enriched his reminiscences of early years in Kingston with the pleasing fact that in his school-boy days he had a part in certain recitations and declamations, then not unusual in your public schools. I have a pleasing recollection of a similar occurrence, a recitation which, as it occurred nearly fourscore years ago, may fairly be set down as my first exhibition of oratory, and as this will probably be my last effort, I might to-day make a sort of *da capo* close, and say, as I then said,

> "You'd scarce expect one of my age
> To speak in public on the stage."

But, sir, I am called up to respond to a sentiment, "The Legends of Kingston." Perhaps other towns in the Old Colony had their legends, and only lacked a historian to give them "form and presence." The descendants of those who yield belief or consent to the narratives of their seniors or the embellishments and additions of their cotemporaries may have forgotten in the tumult of social antagonism for wealth or place, a part or the whole of what had influenced their childhood. But I can bear witness to the fact that in this town almost every rock that guards your bay was deemed at times the residence or resort of the unearthly and the evil; and that the lower, damp portions of land, which then were made dark by exuberant shrubbery, were sacred to spirits that held their ghostly Sabbaths in the shade.

In darkness or in solitude men of stern mould passed through these scenes, consecrated with what you call superstition, in shrinking dread of

"Forms unseen and mightier far than they,"

and occasionally they did homage to the great unseen by acknowledging their existence, which they would rather deny in broad daylight or in a crowd. If it be true that these superstitions have given way to the teachings of reason, and that men, women, and children no longer with awe listen to the stories of what was once a social and practical belief, then, without condemning the past, we may reckon this decay of faith or fear among the changes which are so obvious in Kingston, and to which I shall briefly allude. But before leaving the subject which is the keynote that your committee has sounded, let me say that a belief in the unearthly and of their interference in the affairs of life and in the direction of human beings distinguished all Massachusetts, and certainly it had its mildest form in Kingston where the traditions of witchcraft are not found; though I must confess that I recall the apparition of some beings, whose appearance was so influential that I am not astonished that even in this day, when we ridicule or lament the imputed power of old women witches, we are bound to confess that the spirit has descended to the young, and the charms of cultivated talent and beauty may induce and warrant the admission that witches have not failed from the land.

If the toast by which I am called up had reference to certain literary efforts of my own in which the peculiarities of belief of our native town were the staple of what was written, I can only say that they were the result of early impressions, and, strange to add, they were imparted by an anxious, pious, widowed mother, who, having nothing of worldly wealth with which to endow her eccentric son, was led perhaps by Providence to bestow in her maternal solicitude a love of the marvellous, and to cultivate a habit of fanciful thought, for with the exception of that bestowal,

"When I arrived at man's estate
'Twas all the estate I had."

But wealth would probably have fled or been lost in speculation. The want of that wealth led to constant drafts upon the maternal bestowal, and though you may have profited little by my records of the "Legends of Kingston," yet they became to me the means of some little distinction, and I owe the pecuniary comforts of old age less to the commercial and political stages through which I have passed than to the uses which I made of the legendary lore with which my mother beguiled the hours of my early boyhood.

Though these wild scenes that I have tried to decorate with fancy are not now interesting to you, yet they are classical fields in my remembrance; they are Gardens of Hesperides to my small experience and my inconsequential condition.

"*Paulo majora canamus.*" Let me advance from myself and my doings to remark on some of the changes in Kingston.

Our goodly town was formerly distinguished by the amount of ship-building carried on, on what you called "the landing," — an amount truly great when taken in connection with the dimensions of the river at the points at which the work was performed. That was certainly the life of your place, for almost all other occupations were greatly dependent, directly or indirectly, upon that important specialty. The music of the broad axe, the adze and the mallet, was the daily, unremitted concert from the "flat rock" to the bend of the river, and it was most interesting to look at the hulls of vessels, in every stage of construction, from the day of laying the keel to the bustle of the workmen and the trembling complacency of the master-builder as he gave orders to knock away the "dog shore," which was to allow the mighty fabric to leave the blocks and become a floating palace.

But that music has ceased. Ships are the vehicles of commerce; commerce is the growth of successful trade. When the latter ceases, ships have little use; they are cumbersome, costly possessions. And now your ship-yards, once the scene of so much activity, silently, almost mournfully. await that business change which can alone renew their activity and recall that credit which the genius, the enterprise, and industry of Kingston once made so general.

Another change has come over your town. Not only has shipbuilding ceased, but the use of the small craft in the navigation of your somewhat eccentric river is no longer noticeable. The plan of constructing ships of commerce of iron, of course greatly injured your principal production, and the burning of anthracite coal in domestic uses diminished the demand for cordwood, which made so important an element of the river and coast navigation, and the railroads finished what other new customs began. One consequence of the two changes which I have noticed is most observable; that is the new growth of wood in your interior, so that the deer and other old denizens of your forests have returned to their former haunts in your neighborhood, and wood-craft is likely to take the place of wood-chopping.

It is the true characteristic of genius to rise above the accidents of business, and Kingston, I think, has shown herself eminently capable of great expedients in using those gifts of Providence which had not been made familiar by circumstances. The cessation of shipbuilding, a business that influenced almost all other pursuits among you, and the decay of coast-wise commerce, suspended no hope from individual industry, but rather drew attention to the capabilities which were around. Your enterprise has known how to direct industry into other channels, so that the suspension of one branch of business has led to the adoption of others. The best spirit of the century has been fruitfully operative among you. The multiplied streams, those specialties of your location, which (above tide) seemed only the highway of the migratory denizens of the flood, have been made subservient to the requirements of new industries, and from their sources to their lowest confluents, their power is utilized to the promotion of a multitude of manufactories whose production extends from the ponderous anchor of a majestic ship of war to the small but useful contributions to domestic convenience.

In few pursuits does Kingston present greater advances than in agriculture. I do not know what progress has been made in the production of cereals and other grains, probably not extensive, yet in the production of grasses undoubtedly there have been advances that but for the steadiness of the increase would have caused surprise to your own people. Single large fields now, I am informed, produce more English or artificial grass than was cut in the whole township sixty years ago. This is a true application of science to one of the most important of your industries; and if "he is a public benefactor who makes two blades of grass grow where only one had been raised," certainly a good many people of Kingston in more ways than one swell the list of philanthropists.

Nor should I overlook the wonderful progress which elementary and practical education has made among you. Beautiful school-houses have taken the place of the airy structures, that, in years past, were devoted to the discipline of candidates for maturity. Few, I believe, ever looked at the old "district school-house," with its "looped and windowed raggedness," without feeling the force of the patriarch's exclamation, "Surely this is an awful place!" The advancing spirit of the people is now wonderfully illustrated in the excellent schools and these productive fields

"Giving blossoms to nature and morals to man."

I have said a word upon the effect which the cessation of shipbuilding and that of conveying hence ship-loads of cordwood have had upon your upland forests. I have a little interest, arising out of events of other times, to ask, What is the effect of the increase of your public schools and of the improvement in the modes of education upon the pliant woods of the low lands? How is it with the birch? "I cannot but remember that such things were and were most dear."

Perhaps opinions upon its applications have undergone practical changes. The good man who administered the birch so lovingly, eighty years ago, was wont to quote, with infinite gravity,

"Just as the twig is bent the tree's inclined."

Well, the twig was bent very often, but I do not remember that any of its recipients were much inclined to its reception.

If the Kingston boys of those and later times deserved and received the flagellations of a good master, what kind of men would they make? That is a natural question. I answer in the language of the great architect's epitaph, "Look around."

It is to the immortal credit of Kingston, and to the honor and profit of her sons, that she never moulded a doctrine to suit a practice; wrong was wrong, whoever was the perpetrator. The bad act she punished, and thus limited its effect; the bad theory she knew would perpetuate offence and foster crime.

Some changes have taken place in your means of public devotion. The small, original church or rather "meeting-house," with its disproportioned steeple and diamond-shaped window-glass, its high pews, the corners of which were surmounted by contrivances to sustain the cocked hats of the male worshippers, gave place to another, distinguished externally by two towers, and internally by extraordinary decorations along the galleries; and that twin-steeple house gave place to the neat and beautiful edifice, whose cross upon the steeple catches the first rays of the rising, and reflects those of the setting sun, telling of the faith of those who rest in its shadow. Two other churches denote the freedom of thought exercised here, and that the restrictive creed of other centuries has given place to a better sentiment, which is not startled at the name of toleration, and demands and enjoys a perfect *right* to be or to do. And Kingston will find that just in proportion as she extends the liberty of religious views and indulges sound and religious freedom will be her harmony and her prosperity. Difference of opinion may be earnestly and sometimes intemperately discussed by men of different creeds; that is undoubtedly an evil, but that evil is incomparably smaller than the heart-burnings and disquietude promoted by dissension among those who are of one profession.

Some one has said that Daniel Webster considered New Hampshire "a good State to leave." Certainly, I think Kingston a good place for a youth to leave. He might lack adaptation of talents to the peculiar requirements of his native town, that kind of ability which her business necessities employ and reward. But it is in another light that I view the advantages to a youth of having come from Kingston. He is likely to take with him some of those simple, pure manners that distinguish the place, some of those unyielding principles of right that he has learned from his parents, and especially those habits of industry and perseverance that he has seen in constant illustration by his seniors. He may, indeed, fall into error, but he has never been taught that those errors may be justified. Surely, Kingston has been honored by such emigrant youth, whose after-fame has been part of her boast to-day, and by some whose later liberality has added to your means of high usefulness and beautiful charity. The admirable High School building, that decorates another part of your town, is due to the local love of a son of Kingston; and a charity that distinguishes only between the needy and the possessor is due to the enlarged benevolence of one who went poor from this place, taking with him the simple habits of his virtuous ancestry and the pure principles of his townsmen. I knew him and loved him in his infancy and childhood and followed with deep interest his manly steps, and was delighted to think he was our townsman.

> "But greater gifts were his, a happier doom,
> A brighter genius and a purer heart,
> A fate more envied and an earlier tomb."

Kingston has produced distinguished men, but none of them ever forgot his birthplace; none of them ever felt a breeze of praise or prosperity but he was delighted to think it reached his native town. In peace or in war her children have done their part in social or public service, and pointing to them and to Kingston the world may say,

"This man and that man were born in her."

Others will do justice to the exalted work of those who were born in Kingston and maintain their residence. Your orator to-day has done justice to men who in the hour of trial offered their services and themselves to the nation's good. The very prosperity of your town amid the prevailing gloom of decayed commerce and paralyzed enterprise, the happy hearths, the smiling edifices, and the fruitful fields show that while men of genius and activity were carrying out the means of wealth for themselves they felt and enjoyed the beautiful consequences to others which their own gallant enterprise was diffusing.

The very spot on which your festivity is held affords a most splendid outlook, for, from this very pavilion we may survey the historical points of river and bay, and catch a view of the houses of Cobb and Bradford, that seem to defy (as did the former) the tooth of time. Those hills beyond the gurgling first brook are associated in my recollection with the pleasure and profit of summer exercise. There, a surface wealth abounded which was more valuable in the domestic economy of a virtuous, quiet neighborhood than that which the Black Hills of the Sioux Country is said to afford. There in its season the industry of the young gathered the hills' annual tribute of succulent huckleberries, of which one of your New England poets has sung that they are

"Great in a pudding, glorious in a pie."

The love of my native town has existed and strengthened with many years of absence and often with many leagues of distance, and while I have enjoyed the recollection of her interesting scenery, I have enriched that recollection with the memory of those who made that scenery most dear. If few or none of them are left, their successors have an easy task to build their own credit upon the solid virtues derived from their predecessors. With the recollections of such an exigent soil and such scenery and the knowledge of the actors, it is natural for the absent, in indulging their pride of early home, to exclaim,

"Low lies the land and rocky is the soil,
Her sons are honest and her daughters fair."

That sun which now in unclouded majesty is sinking below the western horizon has never witnessed in this place such a ceremony as it smiles upon to-day. Half a century hence it will shine upon a celebration, influenced by the same motives and sanctified by the same emotions of gratitude to man and praise to God. There will be no changes there but the change of improvement. Other forms may be consistent with future celebrations, but what we love and what we laud will be the stimulants. It will be Kingston, represented as now in her children, sending up anthems of thanksgiving.

The uses of your possessions may alter, and agriculture change yet more the face of your fields, and these affect the forms and locations of your dwellings, but time will not be a destroyer. The rugged rocks that give denomination to a portion of your territory are almost indestructible. And those lovely streams and beautiful lakes that characterize your town and give their names to their locations, shall not be changed. The lakes will for centuries reflect the blue sky from their placid bosoms, and the streams with their charming cadence shall know no cessation,

> "They run and will forever run."

---

6. The Sons of Kingston in the State of Maine, — Stars of the East, the horizon adorning.

RESPONDED TO BY REV. WILLIAM A. DREW, OF AUGUSTA, ME.

Mr. President, — I am here to-day on a revisit to the home of my childhood; to the scenes of beauty which first touched the springs of joy in a young heart; and to recall the welcomed memories of a bright morning in life's opening day, — a day which, with the varied experiences of good and evil, has now entered the evening shadows of a setting sun. And if in the remarks I propose to offer, there should appear anything betraying the imbecility of age, I trust my native townspeople and many kindred present will pardon something to the playful spirit of the period I could wish to recall.

It is an old proverb, which dame Nature herself endorses, that the *genus homo* is "once a man and twice a child." Of course, then, he must have two *nativities*. I may, therefore, claim the singular honor of having two birthplaces, — one in Kingston, Mass., and one in Augusta, Me. This peculiarity, after all, is not so absurd as was the claim of the honest Hibernian who demanded the right to vote for Gov. Rice or some other Democrat (!) because, having lived in Boston twenty-one years, he had become a "native American" since he left Ireland.

I was never ashamed of my first birthplace; I always loved old Kingston. It was here my eyes first opened to the light of day; it was here those sacred affections were formed which will endure forever. I can say as the Hebrew bard said of *his* Jerusalem, "If I forget thee, O Kingston, let my right hand forget her cunning. If I do not remember thee, let my tongue cleave to the roof of my mouth," and with the more modern British poet, —

> " Where'er I roam, whatever lands I see,
> My heart, untravelled, still returns to thee."

True, as a septuagenarian, my second childhood commenced in Augusta. Nor am I ashamed of *that* birthplace. It is a beautiful city, and the capital of that great State, the families in which, the sentiment just offered calls on me to represent.

Daniel Webster, a native of the Granite State, after he removed to Boston, said New Hampshire was a good State to go *from*. The emigrants from Massachusetts to Maine have found that a good State to go *to*. Indeed, before the "Great West" was discovered in the then far-distant valley of the Mohawk, "Down East" was about the only land of promise to which the Old Colony boys could go, to better their condition. The lands were largely owned by the Commonwealth and by rich proprietors at home. A large part of one township, now the town of Turner, was owned by Hon. Wm. Sever, of Kingston, at whose instance it was settled by several of the Gov. Bradford families. Another township, or a large part of it, given by the legislature to Gen. Peleg Wadsworth, of Kingston, for his Revolutionary services, was settled by him, to which, on its incorporation, he gave the name of "Hiram," in honor of Hiram Abiff, the architect of Solomon's Temple, and the first Grand Master of Freemasons, to which order Gen. Wadsworth belonged. Many Plymouth County families are scattered all over the State, not a few of whom bear the Kingston names of Bradford, Brewster, Cushman, Prince, Adams, Wadsworth, Bryant, Holmes, Washburn, Stetson, Cobb, Mitchell, Dunham, Fuller, Bartlett, and Drew. Some of these names have risen to high honor in State and Nation, and all, with some exceptions, have proved themselves good and useful citizens. I never knew of but one Drew that was hung; but he, fortunately for the Old Colony family, belonged to a tribe in New Hampshire that never saw Kingston. That execution took place in Portland shortly before I entered Maine, and subjected me sometimes to the humiliating question, What relation was he to me? I could only say that he stood in the same relation to me that he did to the Adam family which originated in Mesopotamia, the father of which made a lady whom Milton described as "daughter of God and man, accomplished Eve," the mother of *all* the human race. Our relation, therefore, was very distant.

Before I proceed, Mr. President, to fulfil the main object of your call, will you allow me to add a few words more, personal to myself? Having been born almost under the shadow of Forefathers' Rock, it is natural enough that I should claim a relationship to the forefathers themselves and cherish a filial respect for the principles which governed them and which are the foundation of the civil and religious liberties of the New World. Though I do not subscribe to *all* the "five points" in their creed, I do believe that the religion of the Puritans *was* the "purest" which the Christian world has seen since the days of the apostles of Christ, and that it is to the departure from the strictness of that religion that there is at the present day such a decadence in public virtue and private morals as must sooner or later subvert the glory of our republican institutions. If there is a spot on earth where that religion should be revived and extended in its "purity," it is on what Mrs. Hemans calls this "holy ground" of the Pilgrim Fathers on which we now stand.

I said I could claim relationship to the forefathers. The

blood of Elder Brewster circulates in my veins, and it is, perhaps, this hereditary instinct that has inspired my veneration for his religion, and made me, what he was, a minister of the gospel of Christ. Though I claim no other blood relation to the Pilgrims, I think I can say what no other person present or elsewhere can say, viz., that there is but one life between me and the poop-deck of the "Mayflower" that brought the Pilgrims here, having myself been with a man who had enjoyed the caresses of Thomas Clark, the supposed mate of that ship. If the descendants of the centenarian, "Grand'ther Cobb," of Rocky Nook do not challenge a solution of this enigma, perhaps my friend, Dr. Drew, who is the genealogist of our family, may be able to explain how a guest at this table, two hundred and fifty-six years after the landing of the Pilgrims, can be reckoned, in matters of time rather than of blood, as a child of the second generation from the cabin of the Mayflower, — a mere grandson of the foreparents of New England. * He will have, however, to credit tradition for one of the links in the chain of facts.

And now a little more about the Maine State and the Kingston families in it. Half a century ago it was a common idea in Beacon Street, that "Down East" was the very jumping-off place of creation, to which, if a Bostonian should go in the darkness which always rested upon it like a cloud, he would be in danger of pitching off into nowhere, as the Pope told Columbus he would if he ventured ten leagues west of the Pillars of Hercules. The land, which had little or no agricultural value, was supposed to be bound in almost perpetual ice; the people but half civilized, in constant dread of tigers and bears, and subsisting on wild meats and rye johnny-cake. Why, even since I have

---

* E. Cobb, born 1694; T. Clark, died 1697; W. A. Drew, born 1798; E. Cobb, died 1801.

lived there, I have been inquired of by people in Massachusetts, when I have revisited my native State, to know whether corn, one of our surest crops, could grow in Maine, and how the inhabitants contrived to survive the rigors of our Arctic winters. Why, dear souls! don't you know that the Dirigo State is as large as all the rest of New England; that her soil is, on the average, better than that of the parent State, many parts of it being not inferior to the boasted prairies of the West; that our farmers can raise all the necessaries and many of the luxuries of life; that she has more sea-coast, more safe harbors, more navigable rivers, more water-power, and builds more ships than any other State in the Union; that her mineral wealth in granite, lime, feldspar, slate, and iron is inexhaustible, and that her shipments of lumber and ice bring wealth to her very doors; that her people are intelligent, industrious, *temperate* (to the great sorrow of distillers and rumsellers), and as highly educated and loyal as any people in the Union? Why, sir, as to that being a benighted region, don't you know that all the light you have comes first from us; and that some unseen power Down East has to pry up the sun every morning to bless the people of Massachusetts with his smiles *after* we have breakfasted in his light?

And then as to scholars and statesmen: Have you never heard of that Kingston grandson, Henry Wadsworth Longfellow, the poet, whom the Emperor of Brazil came all the way from Rio Janeiro to see and dine with last week? And Grenville Mellen and B. B. Thatcher, hardly inferior to Prof. Longfellow? If the Maine *nom de plume* "Florence Percy" is not the equal of Mrs. Hemans, no American lady is. Who, too, has not heard of Rev. S. F. Smith, author of the National Hymn, "America," sung already at this table? of the celebrated songstress, Alice Cary, and the Peakes family? of the historical

Abbotts and Williamsons? of the scholarly acquirements of Pres. Woods and Dr. Jenks, and of Profs. Cleaveland, Upham, Newman, and Smyth? of George D. Prentiss and Seba Smith, the veritable "Jack Downing of Downingville"? One of Kingston's sons, Dr. Ezekiel Holmes, and two of her grandsons, C. L. Stetson, Esq., of Auburn, and Hon. William P. Drew, of Augusta, have been professors in colleges. Where will you hear of better jurists than Chief Justice Parker, who adorned the Supreme Court of Massachusetts so long; and of Mellen, Wilde, Whitman, and of Greenleaf in the law chair of Cambridge? Where of more distinguished divines than Payson, Appleton, Pond, Nichols, Boardman, Bishop Soule, Bishop Burgess, and Dyke? Where of abler statesmen than King, Parris, Evans, the two Fessendens, Holmes (one of Kingston's most distinguished sons), Gov. Andrew (your own John A.), a whole *family* of Washburns, Gen. and Gov. Chamberlain, to whom the rebel Gen. Lee surrendered the "lost cause," and, though last not least, James G. Blaine, who came as near the presidency as Webster or Clay, and failed for the same reason?

By the Kingston families in Maine I suppose it is not only proper to represent those who still bear the patronymic of the first settlers, but also those who, by intermarriage, have become lawful members thereof; and of these it is respectful to remember not only the first generation, but also the grand and even the great-grandsons and daughters now upon the stage. All this, indeed, would embrace a list too numerous to be detailed here.

Within the family circle thus described, I take pleasure, in honor to old Kingston, to say she has given to the country one senator in the Congress of the United States, Hon. John Holmes, who was the author of the Constitution of Maine;

four representatives in the National Legislature, viz., Gen. Peleg Wadsworth, who represented Cumberland District both in the Continental and Federal Congress; Hon. Joshua Cushman, a lineal descendant of Elder Thomas Cushman; Hon. John Holmes, afterwards transferred to the Senate already mentioned, and Hon. T. J. D. Fuller, of Washington County, who, as I have been assured, originated in one of the Fuller families in Kingston; one governor, and one regular candidate for governor, who failed only for the want of an actual majority of votes, viz., Dr. E. Holmes, the founder and editor of the "Maine Farmer"; one United States Minister to a foreign Court, viz., Hon. John Holmes Goodenow, grandson of Senator Holmes; three judges, Hon. Job Prince, of Turner, Hon. Bezar Bryant, of Anson, and Hon. H. C. Goodenow, of Bangor, brother of the minister at Constantinople; one Secretary of State, Col. F. M. Drew, of Augusta; one adjutant-general, J. P. Cilley, of Thomaston; six State Senators, Hon. Joshua Cushman, of Winslow, Hon. Job Prince, of Turner, and his brother, Hon. Noah Prince, of Buckfield, both of whom were presidents of that Board, Hon. L. L. Wadsworth, of Pembroke, Washington County, and one whom I am happy to see here to-day, Hon. Henry H. Burgess, of Portland, who "escaped a great mercy" by the lack of two votes to make him president of the Senate and thus lieutenant-governor of the State; a large number of local representatives, one of whom was speaker of the House, and two members of the Executive Council, viz., Hon. Benj. Bradford, of Livermore, and Hon. L. L. Wadsworth, of Pembroke.

To this list, by a pardonable license, might be added three *adopted* sons of Kingston families, viz., Gov. Albion Keith Parris, though born in Maine after his father, Judge Samuel Parris, removed thither, was in early youth educated by his and my uncle, Rev. Martin Parris, of Kingston, and was married to the daughter of Rev. Levi Whitman, also of this town. This gentleman, a lawyer by profession, had advanced to more official honors than any man in Maine, having been Senator with Hon. John Holmes, in the Massachusetts Legislature, before the separation, representative in Congress, Governor of the State several years, Judge of Probate, Judge of the Supreme Court, Judge of the District Court of the United States, Senator in Congress, and second Auditor of the treasury in Washington, where he died in office. His was the remarkable case of a successful office-seeker, honest and faithful in every post of duty. Till death he retained his early love of Kingston by constant visits to his uncle and father-in-law, whom he greatly comforted and supported in his needy old age. Hon. Ezekiel Whitman, of Portland, was the adopted son of the same Rev. Levi Whitman, who reared him to manhood and gave him a college education. The relation of father and son was always sacredly respected between them. He was a very distinguished lawyer, twice a representative in Congress from Cumberland County, afterwards an eminent judge and chief-justice of the Supreme Judicial Court of Maine. Hon. Jonathan Cilley, of Thomaston, a lawyer of note, married the daughter of Hezekiah Prince, Esq., of that town, — a Kingston emigrant, — by whom he had a son who was colonel of a Maine regiment of cavalry in the late Rebellion, and who is now adjutant-general of the State. He, therefore, is one of Kingston's grandsons. His father, whilst in Congress, fell in a duel with Graves, of Kentucky.

> "No farther seek his merits to disclose,
> Or draw his frailties from their dread abode.
> There they alike in trembling hope repose,—
> The bosom of his Father and his God."

Though the names I have mentioned had acquired official distinction, I would not have it understood that those in more humble life, past and present, have not done as much in *their spheres* of duty, to confer honor upon the land of their nativity. They constitute now a large and highly useful and respectable portion of the citizens of our State.

" Honor and shame from no condition rise,
Act well your part, there all the honor lies."

The beautifully executed card of invitation issued by your committee, which has brought us together to a celebration just *fifty per cent* more timeworthy than the National Centennial now in progress in Philadelphia (a show which, great as it is, has less attractions for me to-day than the present joyous festival, since my curiosity in such exhibitions was gratified to satiety at the World's Fair in London), gave us the assurance that "the occasion will be one for many pleasant reminiscences and reunions." The "reminiscences," indeed, are fresh and replete with interest, but in the matter of "reunions" there are few who have come here in their second childhood, like myself and my dearly venerated foster-brother from Philadelphia, HON. JOSEPH RIPLEY CHANDLER, and even the senior of us both, the respected nonagenarian, REV. JOB WASHBURN of Camden, Maine, that can participate in that part of the promised pleasure. The "reunion" can, to the most of us, be only in spirit with the spirits of the departed, whose graves we must visit ere we bid this, our last adieu, to our native borough.

Of our cotemporary schoolmates, I am privileged to-day to find but three of my ancient associates, viz., two boys and one girl, or to speak more deferentially, two old men and one old woman; and as we are brought together late in the evening of life, dozing for a final repose, I need not say that Mrs. Caudle's

Curtain Lecture must be short, and take its inspirations chiefly from the land of "Pleasant Dreams."

> "When shall we" *four* "meet again?"
> "When shall we" *all* "meet again?"
> . . . .
> "When the dreams of life are fled,
> When its wasting lamp is dead,
> When in cold oblivion's shade,
> Beauty, fame, and power are laid;
> Where immortal spirits reign,
> "There may we" *all* "meet again."

In parting, now, from these companions of a blithesome boyhood, I may be permitted to recall the memory of one of our schoolmates, now no more on earth, who was, I think, the most precocious scholar, and a thorough one too, of which American history gives a record. I allude to my cousin, SAMUEL B. PARRIS, son of Rev. Martin Parris, our old schoolmaster, who was born in Kingston, Jan. 30, 1806. Before he was eighteen months old he had learned the Hebrew alphabet, and became the master of that sacred language before he studied the English grammar. At the age of six he commenced a diary or journal, in which he recorded the experiences of every day, *confessing all his faults in Latin*. He entered college when only nine years old, being so childlike that he sat in the lap of his professor whilst undergoing a successful examination in the classical languages and the higher mathematics. "Whom the gods love, die young." He died at the age of twenty-one. An interesting volume, entitled "Parris's Remains," was published after his death, containing specimens of his writings both in prose and poetry, alluding, as I also do to-day, to the scenes of our early pleasures. I add only a brief quotation from his poem on "Anticipations and Recollections."

> "Scenes of early pleasure! years may pass,
> In life's united tragedy and farce;
> But, with oblivion's besom, ne'er shall they
> Sweep thy remembrance from my thoughts away."

Only once more: Not only can Kingston claim to have given birth to that remarkable scholar just mentioned, but it is a subject of pride to all her sons that this small but ancient town has contributed more than an average share to the elements of a *national* reputation.

On this shore the forefathers of New England laid the foundations of our national glory. Then Jones River was as much Plymouth as Town Brook. Here Gov. Bradford, his son, the Deputy-Governor, William Jr., Gov. Prence, Dr. Fuller, and Elder Cushman had estates and homes. Here the captain in King Philip's War, Major W. Bradford, led the forces which conquered and killed that powerful Indian monarch. In time of the Revolution, Kingston furnished two distinguished major-generals of the army, the companions of Washington, — Thomas and Wadsworth. Here, in Drew's ship-yard, the first armed brigantines of the Continental Navy, the "Independence" and the "Mars" were built, and were successively commanded by Simeon Sampson, the first naval captain commissioned by the Provincial Congress. Here, in time of the Adams-Franco War Commodore James Sever commanded the frigate "Congress." Here Deacon Jed. Holmes made the first anchors for the navy. Here Jesse Reed invented the first nail and tack machines. Here John Washburn's genius gave the world the benefit of the first and all succeeding screw augers. Here Samuel Adams invented and patented the first mowing machine. In mechanical as well as in patriotic and literary history, therefore, Kingston is entitled to a reputation not to be overlooked on this anniversary, and in which we all may take an honest pride. *Esto perpetua!*

Mr. President, Ladies and Gentlemen,—Thanking you very respectfully for the indulgence by which you have allowed me to trespass so long upon your time and patience, I will only add my parting benediction, GOD BLESS OLD KINGSTON FOREVER! *Farewell.*

---

7. The public schools of Kingston, — best known by their products, — MEN and WOMEN.

RESPONDED TO BY LETTERS.

NORMAL, ILLINOIS, June 24, 1876.

MR. W. R. ELLIS,
 Toastmaster, Kingston Anniversary Celebration:

Dear Sir, — Finding it impossible to be present at your celebration and respond to a toast at your public dinner, I venture to send the following sentiment:

Illinois sends cordial greeting to the Old Colony; the Father of Waters to Jones River; Lake Michigan to Smelt Pond; the luxuriant prairie to the sandy sea-shore; the home of Abraham Lincoln to Abraham's Hill.

May the cable forever remain unbroken which moors the fair Valley of the Mississippi to Plymouth Rock!

Trusting that your celebration will prove eminently successful, I am
  Very truly yours,
    ALBERT STETSON.

SOUTH DARTMOUTH, June 16, 1876.

MESSRS. STETSON & FAUNCE,
 Of the Committee of Invitations, etc.

My dear Sirs, — Please accept my grateful thanks for your very polite and courteous invitation to be present and participate in the " proposed celebration of the one hundred and fiftieth anniversary of the incorporation of Kingston."

It will be a sad occurrence which can prevent me from availing myself of the opportunity of visiting the home of my childhood on the 27th inst., and participating in the exercises of the day.

Yours very truly,
FRANCIS D. BARTLETT.

NEW YORK, June 20, 1876.

MESSRS. STETSON, PECKHAM, SAMPSON, FAUNCE, ETC.,
Committee of Invitations, etc.

Gentlemen, — Your very cordial invitation to revisit my old home and join the present citizens in celebrating the one hundred and fiftieth anniversary of the incorporation of Kingston was duly received.

I regret that I cannot enjoy the occasion with you, but allow me to thank you for your kind invitation and the honorable mention you give me in this connection. It would afford me rare pleasure to join you and others on the 27th inst. I fancy that I am not the less patriotic though a non-resident.

Kingston as a part of the old Plymouth town has certainly a rightful claim to most honorable mention as a constituent factor of this republic in this centennial year.

If the sky be now "HAYES-Y," the guiding star of our national destiny shall so clarify the atmosphere that, as a planet of the first magnitude, this great republic shall lead the nations onward to a purer national life.

Again thanking you,

I remain fraternally yours,
GEO. B. ROBBINS.

WALTHAM, MASS., June 19, 1876.

KIMBALL W. STETSON, ESQ.

Dear Sir, — A few days ago I received from your committee a circular of invitation, extended to natives of Kingston, to participate in the celebration of the one hundred and fiftieth anniversary of the incorporation of the town.

Of course my absence would not be noticed, yet I cannot let the occasion pass without expressing my sincere regrets that other engagements will keep me away from the celebration; examinations and exhibition of my school coming on the 28th or 29th.

The new settlers of the West used to say with virtuous pride that Massachusetts was an excellent State to emigrate from. So we can truly say that no firmer foundation could one wish than old Plymouth Rock and the principles which the good Puritan fathers brought to America, and which have descended in such large measure to their descendants in Kingston.

Thanking you for remembering me, and hoping that the event will be in every way a success,

I remain very sincerely yours,

JOHN T. PRINCE.

SAN FRANCISCO, July 14, 1876.

TO THE COMMITTEE OF INVITATION AND CORRESPONDENCE,
*Of the Hundred and Fiftieth Anniversary
of the Incorporation of Kingston.*

Gentlemen, — Allow me, at this late day, to tender my regrets that I could not be with you all at your grand celebration. It was an opportunity that occurs not this once in many men's lifetime; and if the most extraordinary exertions could have availed, rest assured I should not have been long in making them. We "natives" who have adopted California for a home never meet but we inquire for the latest news from Kingston, and one and all look back with a more than ordinary clinging to the scenes of our boyhood.

The latest files of Plymouth County papers have not yet

come to hand, and we are not fully informed as to the stage of glory you were able to reach; but I trust you did not fail to make it a full centennial *and a half*.

Yours very truly,
FRANK J. SYMMES.

---

8. The early ministers of Kingston.

REMARKS OF ELLIS AMES, ESQ., OF CANTON, MASS.

Mr. President, Ladies and Gentlemen, — The announcement by way of reminiscence of the "early ministers of Kingston," with the posting conspicuously of the names of *Stacey, Maccarty, Rand,* and *Willis* upon the sides of this tent in which we assemble to hear the orator, poet, and historian, seems to justify as much of a response as the time will allow.

On November 8, 1717, a tract of land inhabited by John Bradford, Jacob Cook, and thirty-nine others, inhabitants of the part of Plymouth near Jones River, the northeast part of Plympton and the southeast part of Pembroke, was, by an Act of the General Court, set off and incorporated as a precinct, that is, as a parish or religious society, according to the bounds set out in the report of the committee of the General Court, to whom the matter had been referred, and the territory of that parish was subsequently, one hundred and fifty years ago this day, incorporated into the town of Kingston.

Rev. Joseph Stacey, a graduate of Harvard College, of the class of 1719, and a native of Cambridge, was ordained the first minister of the parish, Nov. 2, 1720. Rev. Daniel Lewis, the first minister of Pembroke, preached the ordination sermon, which was printed and published by the unanimous request of the parishioners. That the setting off of the new parish from the first parish of Plymouth was with the approbation of the latter, is manifest by a full preface to that ordination sermon, written and subscribed by Rev. Ephraim Little, then minister of the first parish, in which he greets the rising and development of the new parish, and addresses Mr. Stacey by all the endearing appellations with which one Christian minister can call another.

Of the pedigree of Mr. Stacey and of his connections except at college, before his settlement at Kingston, I am wholly uninformed. Though very abstemious, and taking abundant exercise in fishing and fowling, he died of a fever Aug. 25, 1741.

He left no sermon nor anything else in print by which we may be able to judge of his intellectual powers; and how much of a man he really was can only be inferred from the general character of the clergymen of his age and from his connection with this parish in particular.

His parishioners, on settling here, were nine grandsons and one great-grandson of Gov. Bradford (all men of high personal character), with their families, namely: Major John Bradford, Gershom Bradford, Israel Bradford, Hezekiah Bradford, Perez Bradford, Ephraim Bradford, William Bradford, David Bradford, Elisha Bradford, and John Bradford, Jr. Among his parishioners were Wrestling Brewster, a great-grandson of Elder Brewster, and Francis Cook, a great-grandson of him of the same name, a passenger in the Mayflower with the Cushmans, the Eatons, and more than thirty others with their families, grandsons, and great-grandsons of the forefathers and first-comers in the Mayflower, the Ann, and the Fortune, reminding one of the names upon the roll in iron in front of Pilgrim Hall at Plymouth. At Mr. Stacey's settlement, Samuel Adams, "the last of the Puritans," had not been born, and the very eldest of Mr. Stacey's parishioners in their youth had attended church at Plymouth with Gov. Bradford himself in his old age, and with Miles Standish and others of the Mayflower, and with others of the second generation, such as Elder Faunce, every way equal to the forefathers themselves.

On Jan. 5, 1721, Mr. Stacey's parishioner, Major John Bradford, son of Major William Bradford, deputy governor, and grandson of Gov. Bradford, who had been before a member of the Council Board of the Province, made a deed of gift to Mr. Stacey of two acres of land for his house lot, being the three cornered lot where the road in the centre of the village branches off one way to Boston and the other to Bridgewater, on which Mr. Stacey built his house, which we saw this day on our march to this place elegantly labelled as the house of the first minister, Mr. Stacey.

A learned historian says, How very able must the ministry have been at Plymouth when Gov. Bradford and Elder Brewster, the founders of civil and religious liberty, were among the parishioners! Applying the same test to Mr. Stacey at the time and during the continuance of his settlement here with the grandsons and great-grandsons of the forefathers, we may justly infer that he was possessed of all the learning and talents that this Puritan parish, an offshoot of the great Puritan parish of Plymouth, could desire.

Thaddeus Maccarty, born in Boston in 1721, a graduate of Harvard College, of the class of 1739, was ordained the second minister, Nov. 3, 1742, being himself then just twenty-one years of age. His great-grandfather, Thaddeus Maccarty, of Boston, was a member of the Ancient and Honorable Artillery in 1681, and died in Boston, June 18, 1705, aged sixty-five years, whose widow, Elizabeth, died June 7, 1723, aged eighty-two. His grandfather, Thaddeus Maccarty, the third son of the first Thaddeus Maccarty, was born Sept. 12, 1670.

His father, Capt. Thaddeus Maccarty, was a master mariner, and carried his son, Rev. Thaddeus Maccarty, while a mere boy, several voyages at sea. Rev. Ellis Gray, a distinguished clergyman of Boston, then only twenty-five years of age, preached the sermon at the ordination of Mr. Maccarty, which was printed at the desire of the church in Kingston. Mr. Maccarty was friendly to the famous George Whitefield, who was in 1745 again preaching over the country, but his parish here was nearly all strongly opposed to Mr. Whitefield, which induced Mr. Maccarty to ask his dismission, which was granted, and Mr. Maccarty preached his farewell sermon on Nov. 3, 1745. Mr. Maccarty was settled in Worcester, June 10, 1747, and continued to preach there until his death, July 18, 1785, aged sixty-three years. His farewell sermon here was first printed in 1804, in which it is difficult, at this distance of time, to perceive any allusion to Mr. Whitefield whatever, or that his dismission was from any cause whatever except by mutual consent.

He occasionally afterwards visited Kingston and preached there, and on one such occasion on his return called upon the elder President John Adams, when a young man just out of college, and procured him to go to Worcester as a teacher, and President Adams mentions the name of Mr. Maccarty in his diary of that period.

Besides his farewell sermon at Kingston (never printed in his lifetime) and his sermon preached at Worcester, June 10, 1748, at his instalment in his pastoral office there, Mr. Maccarty published two discourses delivered at Worcester, April 5, 1759, being the day of the public annual fast appointed by authority, and the day preceding the general muster of the militia throughout the province for the enlisting soldiers for the then intended expedition against Canada. His text was

Joab's speech to the hosts of Israel preceding the war of King David with the Ammonites and Syrians, — 2 Samuel, chap. x, verse 12: "Be of good courage and let us play the men for our people and the cities of our God." Besides a sermon in 1768, on the occasion of the execution of one Arthur, and a sermon in 1770 on the occasion of the execution of one Livesey, both printed, Mr. Maccarty preached at Worcester two sermons, both printed, on the occasion of a special fast observed there, as well as in many other towns, on July 14, 1774, on account of the public difficulties of that time, and also a sermon at Worcester, on the 23d of November 1775, a day of public Thanksgiving by appointment of the General Court.

Mr. Maccarty also preached at Worcester, on July 2, 1778, on the occasion of the execution of James Buchanan, William Brooks, Ezra Ross, and Bathshua Spooner, for the murder of Joshua Spooner, the husband of said Bathshua, at Brookfield, on March 1, 1778. This Bathshua Spooner, who conspired with three British soldiers, then prisoners of war, quartered at Brookfield, to murder her husband, by plunging him into a well, was a daughter of Timothy Ruggles, Esq., formerly of Hardwick, a Tory and refugee, who had formerly been speaker of the House of Representatives of this province, and the granddaughter of Rev. Timothy Ruggles, minister of Rochester in this county, for many years prior to his death in 1768, and with whom Mr. Maccarty had doubtless exchanged while minister of Kingston.

Rev. William Rand, born in 1699, son of Mr. William Rand, of Charlestown, and a graduate of Harvard College, of the class 1721 and who had been the settled minister of Sunderland from 1724, into the year 1745, was settled here in the year 1746. Unlike the parishioners of Kingston, the parishioners of Sunderland were attracted by Whitefield, which led to the dismission of Mr. Rand from the parish there.

Mr. Rand was settled in Kingston at the age of forty-seven, and in the full maturity of his intellectual powers. His published sermons, at the ordination of Rev. David Parsons over the third parish of Hadley, now the town of Amherst, on Nov. 7, 1739; at the ordination of Rev. John Ballantine, at Westfield, June 17, 1741; and at the ordination of Rev. Abraham Hill, at Roadtown, now Shutesbury, Oct. 22, 1742, had established his reputation as a preacher. He was assuredly the great opponent of the famous George Whitefield.

On Sept. 10, 1741, the elder Jonathan Edwards, minister of Northampton, a great admirer of Whitefield, delivered a discourse at New Haven, entitled "The Distinguishing Marks of a Work of the Spirit of God applied to that Uncommon Operation that has lately appeared on the Minds of many of the People of this Land; with a Particular Consideration of the Extraordinary Circumstances with which this Work is attended," to which discourse, as printed in one hundred and ten pages, was prefixed by Rev. Wm. Cooper, of Boston, another admirer of Whitefield, a preface in eighteen pages. To this discourse and preface Mr. Rand drew up an answer, entitled "The Late Religious Commotions in New England considered," in twenty pages to Mr. Cooper's preface, and in forty pages to Mr. Edwards' discourse, which answer was printed in 1743.

This answer was undoubtedly the ablest argument against Whitefield that appeared in print; and the reader will find there, logically written, the whole that can be said against Whitefield's preaching, and against preaching that is sensational and addressed to the passions and to the imagination.

Mr. Rand's answer cannot be abridged so as to be appreciated. I cannot help quoting, however, on page 6 of the reply to the preface, the following words of Mr. Rand: "He," that is,

Mr. Whitefield, " made great pretensions to extraordinary communion with God and Christ, and placed himself high in their favor. 'My Master hath sent me,' 'What shall I tell my Master?' 'I will tell my Master,' 'I will rise up against you at the last day,' were phrases often in his mouth; and they, with some others that he used, were very striking to vulgar minds."

Sixteen clergymen of Hampshire County, of whom Rev. Wm. Rand, of Sunderland, was one, assembled at Springfield on the fifteenth day of February, in the year 1745; and upon conferring together, drew up and subscribed an address to Mr. Whitefield, in which they tell him that his coming to that part of the country was offensive to them; that they knew no justification for his travelling from one place to another, as he had done, to preach where the gospel was already truly and faithfully preached, and that by men, most of whom he, without a great degree of modesty, might esteem better than himself; that he had delivered many false and dangerous doctrines; that he discovered a very censorious spirit by slandering the ministers of the country; and that though many of his errors had been faithfully laid before him, he had not made Christian satisfaction, nor was there then to them any appearance of his reformation; that, as he had disturbed the peace of their churches by the errors he had propagated and by the slanders he had uttered, they looked upon him as a person whom, in God's word they were directed to mark and avoid, as having caused divisions and offences contrary to the doctrine they had learned of Christ; and that they judged it would be of great service to him if he could be persuaded to look more critically than he had yet done, and seriously to review his own conduct; that this might be a means to discover to him his errors and misconduct; that while he continued such as he now appeared to be, they thought it their duty to use their influence to dissuade their people from attending his ministry.

Any one acquainted with the style of Mr. Rand will instantly declare his opinion that this address was chiefly composed by him. This address was subscribed by Rev. Mr. Hopkins, of West Springfield, as leader; by Rev. Mr. Doolittle, of Northfield, second; and by Mr. Rand of Sunderland, third; and by the ministers of Sheffield, Blanford, Brimfield, Stockbridge, and Deerfield; by the two ministers of Springfield; by Rev. Noah Merrick, grandfather of the late Hon. Pliny Merrick, of our Supreme Judicial Court, then the minister of Wilbraham; by the ministers of Westfield, Suffield (then in Massachusetts, but now in Connecticut), and by the ministers of Bernardston, New Salem, and Shutesbury. The publication of this address, signed by Mr. Rand, and well-known at the time as mainly his composition, doubtless precipitated his dismission from Sunderland.

The president, professors, and tutors of Harvard College, an association of ministers convened at Weymouth, on Jan. 15, 1745, the pastors of the church in Brookline, and of the two churches in Roxbury, the ministers of Barnstable County, and of the North Association in the county of Hartford in the colony of Connecticut, in the same year, addressed Mr. Whitefield to the same effect. The venerable Nathaniel Stone, of Harwich, then seventy-eight years of age, the same year, interrogated Mr. Whitefield whether he had any evidence whatever of what he had alleged, viz., that the then ministers of New England were inefficient and incompetent compared with their predecessors sixty years before; and in the next paragraph Mr. Stone declared to Mr. Whitefield that he well knew their predecessors sixty years ago, and had opportunity to observe, and had observed them, and that on comparing them, the present clergymen were as lively a ministry as the former; and in the address of the association of ministers at Weymouth they declare that in almost every town where Mr. Whitefield had preached, the consequence had been an alienation between the minister and people.

No wonder that Mr. Rand should be sought for and settled by the parishioners of Kingston, who were so unanimous in their opposition to Mr. Whitefield. Mr. Rand's sermon at the ordination of Rev. Charles Turner, at Duxbury, on the 23d of July, 1755, was published; as also his charge to the Rev. Caleb Gannett, at his ordination in Hingham for Cumberland, Nova Scotia, in 1767; and at the ordination, in Duxbury, of Rev. Zedekiah Sanger, in the year 1776.

It is a decisive evidence of the learning and talents of Mr. Rand, and of the estimation in which he was held by the clergymen of this State, at that period, that he was elected to preach and did preach the sermon to the ministers of the Massachusetts Bay in New England, at their annual meeting in Boston, on the 26th day of May, in the year 1757, which was published.

Rev. Zephaniah Willis, the fourth minister of Kingston, a graduate of Harvard College, of the class of 1778, was the only son and child of Mr. Zephaniah Willis, of Bridgewater, whose great-grandfather, John Willis, Esq., emigrated from England, and was a resident at Duxbury as early as 1637, became an original proprietor of Bridgewater, and settled there as early as 1656, when that town was incorporated; was its first representative to the Legislature of the Colony of Plymouth in 1657, and from that time to 1681, including the period of King Philip's War was that town's representative, — seventeen years more; was justice of the peace, and a man on whom the town much relied, who died at West Bridgewater, Aug.

27, 1693, as see in the Probate Records at Plymouth, Vol. 1, page 146, where we find his will proved Sept. 20, 1693.

A lineal descendant from John Willis, Esq., I claim a remote relationship to Rev. Zephaniah Willis. I own fifteen acres of land in West Bridgewater, parcel of the large landed estate that descended to him through his father from John Willis, Esq., one of the original proprietors of the territory of ancient Bridgewater. Rev. Mr. Willis sold out his inheritance in Bridgewater when he settled in Kingston. He was many years one of the trustees of the Bridgewater Academy, and I was examined by him as such trustee in the latter part of August, 1823, at the examination of the scholars who had attended school at the term then closing. On being informed that I had read through the Æneid of Virgil, he casually opened at the beginning of the Fifth Book, and called upon me to construe. I quickly found myself in the hands of a sharp critic of the Latin language. As one instance of a number of his criticisms then: In the third line of Book V, I construed to him the words "*mœnia respiciens*," and rendered them "beholding the walls," to which he replied that true Æneas was beholding the walls, but that the word "*respiciens*" signified "looking back upon," and that as Æneas was sailing away from "the walls which shone with the flames," the word "*respiciens*" was the word which indicated precisely what Æneas was doing. There are so many present that well knew Mr. Willis personally, that I might leave off in the middle, or even at the beginning, as to him.

He that knows not something of the biography of the ancient ministers of the parishes of New England, graduates of Harvard and Yale to a great extent, is deficient in his knowledge of the history of our country. They had great influence upon the affairs of the community in their age. The legislators of their time in the Colonial and Provincial General Assemblies looked up to them and sought their advice at the crises of the nation's peril. The learning and intellectual productions of the ancient ministers have long ago become mixed up with and become part of the common learning and intelligence of the people of the country, and the fair fame of the first four clergymen of Kingston is without blemish, stands high, and will grow brighter and brighter unto the perfect day.

---

9. Kingston, having furnished two Presidents of the Old Colony Railroad Company,* rejoices to-day in the presence of another of her successful sons, who is a Railroad Commissioner of the State. Before the train starts to bear our honored guest to his adopted home, we hope to hear from him.

RESPONDED TO BY HON. FRANCIS M. JOHNSON, OF NEWTON.

Mr. President, Ladies and Gentlemen, — Talfourd has said, a scent, a note of music, a voice long unheard, the stirring of the summer breeze, may startle us with the sudden revival of long-forgotten feelings and thoughts. How rich in reminders of the past is this occasion! It is now twenty-seven years since I left Kingston and took up my abode among strangers; but memory, obeying the commands of the heart, annihilates time and space, and I confront at will the familiar scenes and impressive events of other days, — the days when Kingston was my home. The view is panoramic, and every object by its associations is a treasure. I will refer to one or two of them. There stands the old meeting-house, where I attended Sunday School and sang second treble in the choir. I see its spacious portico, and two quaint cupolas, each surmounted with a gilded ball, and its solemn-toned bell,— how hearts have ached when that bell has tolled! — the high, white pulpit, occupied successively by parsons Willis, Cole, Sweet, and

* Col. John Sever and Alexander Holmes.

Pope; the galleries on either side, and the singing seats opposite the pulpit, provided with curtains, behind which the younger members of the choir exchanged expressions of friendship, unobserved by the preacher above or the congregation below.

Prominent among the choir stands Deacon Jedediah Holmes, playing most vigorously on the "big bass viol," and Walter Bartlett, leading off with the sharp-toned violin. There are the roomy pews of unpainted pine, topped out with short-turned balusters and rail, and the little box-pew away off in the corner, next the ceiling, for colored folks. But the colored man now, in this centennial year, sits nearer the pulpit than he used to; he has a seat, also, in our halls of legislation. Thanks to those noble men and women who protested against the institution of slavery on the rostrum, and the gallant boys in blue who fought against the slave-power on the field of battle, and vanquished it there, we are able to say of the United States of America what the poet Cowper has said of England, "Slaves cannot breathe in America. If their lungs inhale our air, that moment they are free. If they touch our country, their shackles fall. That's noble, and bespeaks a nation proud and jealous of the blessing. Spread it, then, and let it circulate in every vein throughout this great country, that where Columbia's power is felt, mankind may feel her mercy too."

The old meeting-house gave place to the present Unitarian church in 1851, and according to the historian it was erected in 1798, on the site of one built in 1718. The general appearance of the town has not changed very much in these twenty-seven years, — its picturesque beauty has always been a subject of remark; but who can relate the changes that have taken place among the people, among the families of the town? Here the changes have been great. The silent monuments in the churchyard and cemetery denote this; the busy broods of beings which have sprung into existence, and scattered, as the young birds scatter from the parent nest, all testify to this. The young have become middle-aged, and the middle-aged old; the stripling of thirty years ago is now the orator of the day, with power of speech to stir men's hearts and minds according as he wills. All see and feel the power, the silent, mysterious power, of time.

As I remember, Kingston was progressive, and kicked up as much of a dust as any other town of her size. She had her temperance meetings, and Miller meetings, where was sung

> " In eighteen hundred and forty-three
> Will be the year of jubilee,"

and anti-capital punishment meetings, non-resistant meetings, abolition meetings, and I believe women's rights meetings, beside lyceum lectures and debating societies. I am quite sure the ladies of Kingston held women's rights meetings if they desired any rights they did not possess, for neither the men nor the women of Puritan stock have ever been backward in asserting their rights. Would there not be an immense women's rights meeting, if the Massachusetts legislature should enact the old Roman law of 2,081 years ago? This law read, " No woman shall possess more than half an ounce of gold, or wear a garment of various colors, or ride in a carriage drawn by horses in a city or town, or any place nearer thereto than one mile, except on occasion of some public religious solemnity." This law was repealed at the request of the matrons of Rome and the towns surrounding, who assembled *en masse* at the capitol, and protested against it.

Kingston heard the voices of the best lecturers of the period, such as Phillips, Douglas, Brown, Foster, Gough, and Garrison, and it did not cost *then* $500 to secure a lecturer on any subject.

In "Tippecanoe and Tyler *too*" times Kingston had her log cabin as good as the best of them; and the cry of "Hard cider, $2 a day and roast beef" had, as Josh Billings would say, "its average enticin effect"; for Kingston, like other cities and towns throughout the country, has had a weakness for the allegorical and romantic during the heat of important political campaigns.

The time allotted me is up. I thank you for your kind attention to my bric-à-brac remarks.

---

10. No name has been more prominent in our town than that of Sever. There is a LITTLE bit of history connected with their origin here of special interest to us all.

RESPONDED TO BY THE FOLLOWING LETTER.

NEW YORK, June 13, 1876.

Dear Sir, — Your kind invitation to be present as a guest at the one hundred and fiftieth anniversary of the incorporation of our native town is duly received. I beg you to believe that my inability to accept the invitation is not caused by indifference or by want of love for the dear old town which I delight to claim as my birthplace. It is associated with one of the happiest of boyhoods, and every inch of its ground recalls some youthful pleasure. No day ever passes without my thoughts turning to it. Before me in my study always hangs a picture of my home, — that home which, in vacation days, I always gladly sought until death, by its too frequent comings, taught me that not *houses* but *hearts* make home. The cemetery now is more homelike than any other place, and there, when the work of a busy life is over, I hope to rest.

The first occurrence of the name of Sever in Kingston is

almost coeval with its incorporation. Tradition has it that Nicholas Sever, a graduate of Harvard College, in the class of 1701, and afterwards pastor of a Congregational Church in Dover, N. H., was taking a horseback journey to Cape Cod for the benefit of his health. Arriving at Kingston, he halted on his way at the house of a Widow Little, subsequently owned and occupied by my grandfather, John Sever. Mrs. Little found in the stranger whom she entertained, an angel unawares, and on the 21st of November, 1728, became his wife. She was herself a lineal descendant of the Winslows and the Warrens of the Mayflower. Three sons were born of this marriage, William, James, and John. The two latter died without surviving issue, and William, who lived till June 15, 1809, is still known to the older inhabitants as Judge or Squire Sever. The house now occupied by Miss Jane R. Sever was built for him at the time of his marriage to Sarah Warren, of Plymouth, in 1760. Like his father, he had three sons, William, James, and John. William in early life moved to Worcester, and was the father of the late Mrs. Gov. Lincoln and Mrs. Rev. Dr. John Brazer, of Salem. James was the late Capt. Sever, not yet passed out of memory, and John was my grandfather, who died in 1803, leaving six children, the three eldest of whom, as in the two preceding generations, were named William, John, and James. Those of this later generation who remained in Kingston always, I believe, proved themselves public-spirited citizens, devoted to everything that would promote the honor and welfare of the town. Those who settled elsewhere were always strong in their attachment to their birthplace. The male line of the name in town ceased on the death of my father in April, '69. I am sure that by all the descendants of Nicholas Sever, the name of Kingston will ever be regarded with peculiar reverence and affection.

With many thanks for the kindness shown and the honor done me in your invitation, and with regret that it does not seem expedient to me to accept it,

I am most cordially yours,

WINSLOW W. SEVER.

---

11. Cape Cod, — the right arm of Massachusetts.

RESPONDED TO BY HON. JOHN B. D. COGSWELL, OF YARMOUTH.

It seems to me, Mr. President, eminently proper that, on this occasion, you should remember that picturesque peninsula, without the intervention of which, like an outstretched arm, we should not be gathered together. Most thankfully our fathers welcomed its shelter on that memorable Saturday noon when the shattered Mayflower dropped its anchor in Provincetown Harbor, thirty-five days before the landing at Plymouth. There they refreshed and refitted themselves after the discomforts and perils of the terrible voyage; there they thanked God for deliverance from the dangers of the sea, and with a spirit of cheerful resolution they sang such songs of praise as Deborah and David had sung of old. Dec. 10, Carver, Bradford, and others of the exploring expedition kept the Sabbath on Clark's Island in Plymouth harbor, and their abstinence from labor and journeying has been justly extolled by eloquent tongues; but at the same hour, the main body on board the ship were, for the fifth time, exhorted by Elder Brewster to lift up their eyes and hearts from the beach and hills of Provincetown to contemplate that heavenly country whither they were tending.

Save the sick and the infant in arms, all the Mayflower company pressed the sands and explored the secret places of the cape. Standish, Bradford, and the exploring band encamped two nights in Pamet, now Truro, where they first caught a glimpse of savages, flying before them. There they found the ship's kettle, and the hidden corn which they carried away with them in it and in their pockets, seed-grain for the twenty acres which they planted the next spring, and which gave them "good increase," saving the lives of all at Plymouth. Here, too, they first inspected the architecture and furnishing of the Indian wigwam, and the memorials of the departed, buried in the Indian grave. Sounding along the shore, and exploring the inlets of Wellfleet and Eastham, they were rudely assailed in the dusky dawn of Dec. 8 by that stormy flight of angry arrows which they called the "First Encounter."

In the "Provincetown Roadstead" the question of settlement there had been earnestly discussed, and not the least accurate of their chronicles has asserted that but for the wild snow-storm of Dec. 8, which prevented their seeing the point of Sandy Neck, the permanent settlement would have been made at Cummaquid, now Barnstable. Nor did the establishment at Plymouth cause the fathers to forget the scenes of their temporary sojourn. In the following June they were again at Cummaquid and Mattakeese (Yarmouth), and through the intercession of our courteous sachem, Iyanough, recovered the lost boy from those Nausets who before had greeted them with hostile arrows. Poor Iyanough! Terrified by the loud threats of Standish, he fled into the cape swamps, where he perished of exposure, and his bones, if a learned antiquary is not at fault, are to be seen in the vestibule of Pilgrim Hall yonder. But the "First Encounter" was also the last hostile meeting between the English and the Indians of the cape. They were and even to this day are, friends in peace, allies in war. Gov. Bradford and his successors bought corn and beans of them in various times of dire distress and famine.

By 1627 the Pilgrims had established a trading-post at Manomet, now called Cohasset Narrows, in the present town of Sandwich, the permanent settlement of which commenced in 1637. Sandwich, Yarmouth, and Barnstable had deputies in the General Court in 1639. Duxbury and Scituate alone had preceded these towns in the order of settlement. In 1643 Gov. Thomas Prince, Deacon John Doane, and Edward Bangs led so large a company to Eastham, on the cape, that the church at Plymouth, it was lamented, was left like a mother bereft of her children. Seven times, Prince, "majestic of presence and a terror to evil-doers," was re-elected governor, whilst resident at Eastham.

The last governor of the colony of New Plymouth when it was merged in the Massachusetts — "the calf," as was said, "dying in the cow's belly" — was Thomas Hinckley, of Barnstable. He was not the least meritorious of the six governors. Born at Tenterden, in Kent, England, in 1618, he was only two years old when the Pilgrims landed at Provincetown; but he came over to Plymouth when a lad, and at twenty-one years of age was in Barnstable with Pastor Lothrop and the Scituate Colony. His name appears on the first page of the records of Barnstable, and does not disappear from them till his death in 1706, at eighty-eight years of age, a survivor of the colony by fourteen years. As early as 1745 he was in Plymouth as deputy, was successively assistant, deputy governor, commissioner of the United Colonies, and governor by many annual elections, until by his last official act, proclaiming a fast upon the merger of the Pilgrim Colony with its more powerful Puritan neighbor, New Plymouth ceased to exist. During his time, and especially in the period of the Indian and French Wars of 1775-6 and 1790, much official business of the colony was transacted at Barnstable. He was industrious, devout, a friend to education, firm, acute, astute, skilled and diligent in public business, comprehensive of those arts which make a small State grow large.

I believe this hasty sketch will amply demonstrate that the fourteen towns of the Cape (including the new Indian town of Mashpee) have ample right to participate in the historical festivities of the people of the Old Colony, that noble commonwealth unsurpassed in influence and glory, if the smallest in numbers and the meanest in substance. Indeed, we of the Cape have sometimes thought that the associations, memories, lineage, labors, contributions, and valor, of our immediate ancestry and our birthplace, were sometimes strangely overlooked at Plymouth. But after all, what does it matter? We all have part in that immortal story of sacrifice, devotion, triumph, such as poets and orators are yet unable adequately to recite. Though monuments may never rise and statutes never be erected to the Pilgrims of Plymouth, the earth and the heavens are telling forever their story, more enduring than the marble, more inspiring than architecture.

You, fellow-citizens of Kingston, celebrate to-day the one hundred and fiftieth anniversary of your separation as a municipality from old Plymouth. We of the upper Cape towns are almost ready to celebrate our two hundred and fiftieth. Our ancestors, also, entered in through the gateway of Plymouth. We trace to the Mayflower, to the Fortune, to the Ann, to the Leyden Church, to the church of Jacobs and Lothrop in London, to Pastor Robinson himself; and the precious seed we received, we have kept pure and unmixed with foreign and degenerate. We are more English than England, nay, we are nearer Plymouth than Plymouth itself. But by an instinct of nature, we are all drawn to the cradle of the race, just as we read that the body of William Bradford, the second, was borne through deep snows with great difficulty from his residence near Jones River, because he had expressed a desire to be buried by his father, the second governor, the good and wise historian of New Plymouth.

When I received an invitation to participate in this festival of that part of Plymouth lying upon Jones River, I recalled certain documents I had lately seen in the archives of Massachusetts, having reference to the laying out of a new road over Jones River in 1709, embracing a report of John Otis of Barnstable, grandfather of the famous James Otis and of Mercy Warren of Plymouth, drawn up by the direction of the Barnstable County Court of Sessions. These papers show how intimate was still the connection of our fathers, the Cape people being obliged to contribute to the support of bridges in Plymouth County.

I also found in the archives a petition of Joseph Sampson and others, selectmen of Kingston, dated Aug. 15, 1781, addressed to Gov. John Hancock, "captain-general, etc.," asking that Capt. Daniel Loring may be commissioned captain of "one of those sort of boats commonly called Shaving Mills to cruise on the enemies of the United States," which had been built and equipped by a number of the inhabitants of this town. The document evinces the activity and patriotism of the people during the Revolution, which doubtless still exist; but have you any "Shaving Mills" now? or do you go for them to Boston or to the Banking establishments of our friend, Mr. Davis at Plymouth, and the rest? I will hand these papers to the Committee of Arrangements to be printed, if they shall think them of interest to anybody in this generation.

[Archives of Massachusetts, Vol. 171, p. 460.]

Kingston.

To his Excellency John Hancock Esq.

Capt. General, & Governor in Chief of the Comth of Mass. Bay:

Sir: Whereas a no. of the inhts of this town have built & equipt one of those sorts of Boats commonly called Shaving Mills to cruize on the enemies of the U. S., & are desirous that Cap. Daniel Loring of this town shd. be com^d to command sd. boat, we, therefore, the subscribers, selectmen of the town, beg leave to recommend sd. Loring to yr. Eminency as a person in whose fidelity & prudence, yr. Excellency may put full confidence & pray yr. Excellency wd. grant him a com^n for that purpose.

Kingston, 15th Aug. 1781.

JOSEPH SAMPSON.
JOHN FAUNCE.
JED: HOLMES.

His Excellency John Hancock, Esq.

[Vol. 113, pp. 505-508, Archives of Massachusetts.]

The Court of Gen Sessions of Barnstable County, having been served at its Term of April 1709, with a copy of the pet^n of Samuel Bartlett & David Alden, Selectmen of Duxbury & Saml Sprague & Ephraim Ellis, agents for the Town of Marshfield, relative to the turning of the road or Highway that leads over "Jones River," "directed its clerk, William Bassett, to certify to the General Court, the appointment of Hon. John Otis Esq. of Barnstable, and Mr. John Paine, of Eastham, its representatives, to lay before the General Court " the proceedings that have been relating to the turning said way, and the motives leading thereto," which duty, Messrs. Otis and Paine performed very judiciously on the 3^d of May following, by memorial to the General Court, giving four principal reasons why the location of the road had been changed, upon the application of the town of Plymouth & the Court of Gen Sessions for the County of Barnstable, ie. New way wd. be much better: less chargeable to maintain: the expense & neglect of "Causey" on North side of old bridge: avoids the causey on South side wh. was very low & difficult when the "Tidde" was high: and 4^{thly} new way is 40 or 50 rods shorter through better country, & hath the unanimous concurrence of the Southern inhabitants, "as hath appeared by their cheerful paying of a considerable tax."

Their report proceeds upon the ground of general public benefits to which contrasts the petition of Elisha Wadsworth of Duxborough, "That whereas the justices of the County of Plymouth have seen cause to demolish ye bridge over ye river between ye towns of Plymouth & Duxborough (called Jones River) and to lay out another way which is extremely to my damage. For whereas formerly by opening one gate, I could goe on mine own land to ye Queen's Rode & then I had but four miles to Plymouth Town, and now I have six miles and a half: and one mile further to mill: and also ye situation of my living and ye commodity of my Place, are much Damnified. And further to augment my Grief, my neighbours y^t dwell between me and ye new Rode afores^d, through whose land ye old Rode passeth, have divers times fenced up ye same, so y^t I have been forced to pull it down, before I could pass on my earnest occasions: for wh. they daily threaten to Arrest me, whereby I am in continuall danger, yet notwithstanding, our justices take no care for my relief.

The humble request, y'fore of your grieved supplicant is for such relief &c.

ELISHA WADSWORTH."

Caleb Loring, agent for Plimpton, petitions for that town, in support of the new way.

On the coming Fourth of July I shall have the honor of addressing the inhabitants of the venerable town of Barnstable, upon the Cape; and if opportunity offers, shall not fail to tell them that on this, their happy anniversary, the people of Kingston, once the people of Plymouth, have kindly remembered that our ancestry bore with theirs, the toils, the deprivations, sustained the burdens and faced the perils, the glorious fruitage of which has made the name of "Pilgrim" the most honored among men.

---

12. Our Past; it is studded with memories over which the Historian, Poet, and Scholar love to linger.

RESPONSE BY HON. HENRY S. WASHBURN, OF BOSTON.

Much has already been said, Mr. President, upon the subject which you have assigned to me, but the theme is far from being exhausted. We might, I am sure, indulge in these pleasant remembrances of the past far into the night before us, and yet leave unsaid and unsung much that would awaken the tenderest emotions of our being.

We come together from remote distances to exchange greetings and congratulations, and to look upon forms and faces associated with the recollections of our early days.

> "We tread in olden paths to-day,
> We muse on hallowed memories here,
> And linger fondly by the way
> With friends we've missed for many a year."

I am reminded daily of Kingston by meeting its sons in the streets of Boston, for many years the city of my habitation. You have long been honorably represented there in the persons of several of its most respected citizens. Of these, the president of the day is a worthy illustration. He is not always as staid and sober as you see him now, nor does he usually address me in the dignified manner in which I have just been introduced to you. "How are you, Henry?" and "How are you, Nathaniel?" were salutations which only a few days ago passed between us. How tenderly does this familiar recognition by old friends move us! How much dearer to the heart is it than all the Misters, Esquires, and Honorables, by which the world addresses us! "There is no one left now to call me Victoria," said the British queen on the death of the prince consort. How does this reveal the almost infinite longings of the heart, amid all the glare and blandishments of life, for familiar voices, still calling after us by the name we bore in our childhood! And so to-day we touch the tenderest of chords as we recognize each other as Nathaniel and Joseph, Edward and Levi, Mary and Hannah, Eliza and Rebecca.

I referred to the president a moment ago as one who in Boston had been an honor to his birthplace. An ex-president of the Mechanics' Association, himself an accomplished artisan and builder, it is the pride of his friends to point to some of the most imposing and substantial structures in the city as the product of his skill and genius. And here, by my side, sits another who has just addressed you, a gentleman well-known for his sterling integrity and large business capacity. When, recently, the President of the United States, like Diogenes of old, was searching, with a lantern in his hand, for an honest man to fill the position of postmaster of the city, he selected a Kingston boy, Edward S. Tobey!

Opposite to me, upon this platform, is still another, the possessor of an ample fortune, acquired by his own energy and industry, whose rosy face and benevolent look speak always of peace and good-will to men. As a good steward he rejoices in dispensing to the needy of the abundance which has been given to him. Many a weary one, rising from a bed soft as down could make it, has had occasion to bless the name of Henry R. Glover.

And here, too, I see one, unassuming and unpretending, who, in his own quiet but effective way, is constantly going about doing good. In all our reformatory and penal institutions, the benignant face and venerable form of "Uncle Cook" is daily seen, bringing words of succor and good cheer to those who literally have no one to care for them. Into his ear how often has the Master whispered, "Inasmuch as ye have done it unto one of the least of these my brethren, ye did it unto me"!

Nor let me refrain, Mr. President, in this connection, from referring to him, my honored kinsman, who, in the fulness of years, after having borne the burden and heat of the day, has travelled more than two hundred miles to mingle his congratulations with us on this occasion. At the age of four-score-and-ten years he waits "till the shadows are a little longer grown" before he shall pass away from the scenes and responsibilities of earth. Kingston can boast of few men more worthy to be honored than Job Washburn.

My thoughts involuntarily turn at this moment to another, not now among the living, but upon whom, until recently, you looked with feelings of pride and veneration. I refer to the late Ichabod Washburn, a native of Kingston, a gentleman well-known throughout the commonwealth. And here allow me to relate an anecdote regarding him, which I am sure will interest you. The son of a sea captain, he at an early age, with his twin brother and a sister, sustained the loss of his father, and was thrown upon his own energies for support. His brother had the misfortune to be born with only one arm, and it was deemed best that a portion of the small property left to the family should be expended in giving him an education which would fit him for some one of the learned professions, but that Ichabod should acquire the knowledge of a trade by which to earn his living. Up to that time cotton cloth had been made chiefly on hand-looms, some of which are still to be found in the farm-houses around us. Cotton factories, or the making of cotton by machinery, were just then coming into use. One of the earliest of these institutions was established by Deacon Holmes, in the west part of this town. An opening was presented for the boy Ichabod to work in this factory, which was soberly considered by the immediate friends of the family. The opinion was freely expressed that the position for a while might be a good one; but as these factories were turning out cotton rapidly, it was evident they would soon fill up the world with the article, and the boy would be thrown out of employment. Horses and oxen, however, must always be shod, and iron work of various kinds would be required, and so these wise men thought it would be safer to put him out as an apprentice to learn the trade of a blacksmith. When we consider the crude and imperfect machinery of that day, and compare it with the wonderful mechanism now displayed in the cotton mills of Lowell, Lawrence, and Fall River, we can but smile at the opinion then entertained of a speedy overstock of cotton cloth in the country. But the boy blacksmith faithfully served his master till he reached his majority, when he threw off the shackles that bound him, and struck out for himself as a manufacturer in a department of business which soon led him to fame and fortune. That fortune, honorably acquired, distilled ever as the dews; and it was his pleasure, as you well know, not to overlook, in the distribution of his property, the town of his nativity.

Upon the order of exercises before us is a cut, representing the old church, with two steeples, so well remembered by elderly people present. It may be fitting that I should read a few lines referring to that venerable edifice, which I composed many years ago, but have never published.

THE VILLAGE CHURCH.

It stands where it stood in the olden time,
When my step was light in my boyhood's prime;
And I hear, on the breath of the morning, swell
Again the chime of that old church bell.

It stands where it stood on the brow of the hill,
And the people tread in its old aisles still,
While I look around and inquire, Where
Are the good old men who once worshipped there?

And they point to the grave-yard close by the way,
And they tell me they've been there for many a day;
That the manly heart and the blushing maid
Have been long in that quiet graveyard laid.

Old Meeting House, Kingston, Mass. Built 1798. Demolished 1851.

> There was one I remember; his mild blue eye
> Was wet with tears when he breathed good-by,
> And the clasp of his hand was warm and true;
> But he wasted away like the early dew.
>
> Oh! my heart is sad, old church, while I gaze
> Around for the friends of my early days,
> And my tears fall fast as the April rain,
> For I seek the departed here in vain.

Mr. President, this occasion, which must be interesting to all, is to some of us full of tenderness and significance. After many long and weary years, passed in toil and conflict, we return to find, notwithstanding earth's chances and changes, these hills and vales still the same, the same these dim old woods, these silver streams, these fragrant meadows, this land-locked harbor, and the boundless expanse of ocean spread out beyond it. As a village, quiet and unpretending, comparatively little known in the wide, wide world, its people, from generation to generation, have, as God has given them ability, performed their part in the great drama of life, true and loyal ever to the best interests of their State and the country. Right happy are we to pay our homage at this dear old shrine to-day. If the mother is glad to see her children, they are equally glad to see their mother. If she is proud of her sons, they are also as proud of her. The gladness and the pride are reciprocal.

At the foot of this hill, as you come to the Jones River, in turning into what was once a lane, but now more of a highway, you reach, in a few rods, after passing over a little brook, an old house, which to-day bears an inscription informing us that it was standing in 1703. For the most, if not through all its history, it has been the home of my ancestors. There my father and grandfather were born, and there still resides a cousin of mine, one of the committee of arrangements for this festival. Here, also, my childhood was passed; and I cannot refrain, in closing these remarks, from paying a passing tribute to that dear little stream, so tenderly associated with my boyhood, and which still flows on, beautifying and gladdening the valley through which it passes.

THE BROOK.

There is a brook, a merry brook,
  Whose waters glide away,
And creep within each tiny nook,
  Like a little child at play.

It runs beside my grandsire's door,
  The same as, when a child,
I heard its mimic waters pour
  Their music on the wild.

The passing stranger may not heed
  This modest little rill,
Which wanders through the verdant mead,
  Its pleasant journey still:

But unto me, O stream! a voice
  Hast thou of buried years;
I cannot see thee but rejoice,
  I cannot but with tears.

'T is not because the hills and vales
  Through which thy pathway lies
Are fairer than the hills and dales
  Beneath a thousand skies;

Nor yet because thy waters leap
  So joyously and free,—
No, not for these my heart doth keep
  This memory of thee.

'T is for the past that thou canst stir
  Each passion at thy will,
For halcyon days, that I prefer
  Thy sparkling waters still.

Oh! thou art wedded to the days,
   The blessed days of youth,
When gently fell the loving rays
   Of tenderness and truth;

To the memory of the early dead
   Within their cold graves sleeping;
Thou art, for hours forever fled,
   A thousand memories keeping.

Sad were our being, if the mists
   Of gathered years could hide
The past, that we might not recall
   Who lived, who loved, who died!

Then thanks to thee, thou little rill,
   For the record thou dost bear,
The record of the good and ill
   Which slumbers by thee there.

A pilgrim from the din and strife
   Of earth, I turn to thee.
Full soon must end this checkered life,
   Bear record, then, of me!

---

13. The successful business men who have gone out from our town, as they do not forget us, they will be held in perpetual remembrance by us. Particularly in memory of Ichabod and Charles Washburn of Worcester, Mass.

REMARKS BY CHARLES F. WASHBURN, ESQ., OF WORCESTER.

Ladies and Gentlemen and kinsmen of every degree, — I arise under peculiar circumstances, — to speak of and for those who would have been so happy to be here to-day; to whom Kingston, physically and socially, was dear, was *replete* with interest; to whom, probably, one third of those present were related in some degree by tie of blood. I refer to Ichabod and Charles Washburn, late of Worcester in this State.

Representing, as I do for the moment, natives of this town

who have passed away, I have, while sitting here, been constrained to liken myself to one born of Athenian parents in some Greek colony on the Asiatic shore, who, without having ever before seen the proud city of Minerva, had been made from earliest childhood intensely interested and thoroughly acquainted with its history, and who from the conversation of his parents had grown up with the feeling that his home was Athens and that her people were his people. Such are my feelings for you and for this old town.

This commanding hill is dear to me because from its summit my dear departed ancestors have looked out upon and enjoyed this same grand panorama, — the Gurnet, the spires of Duxbury, Captain's Hill, the mouth of Jones River, Plymouth Harbor, Clark's Island, the ocean-vexed beach, Plymouth itself. Could the foreigner by birth, but Athenian by blood and education, have looked from the Acropolis upon the same number of objects with greater interest than I do upon the objects and scenes I have mentioned, and which were never more plainly to be seen than spread before us on this auspicious day? I trow not! Why, not a place or point have I mentioned, associated with which I have not more than one narrative or anecdote from the lips of my father or uncle.

And just here let me say that while, though the story of Salamis and its victory would be sweet to our Athenian, the story of Clark's Island and its victory is to-day just as dear to me. Yes, more important in its results, grander in its purpose, was the single act of our chilled, jaded, storm-tossed forefathers, in deciding to remain on Clark's Island that first Sunday, *because it would be breaking the Sabbath* to move to the blessed main land, than ever was that successful onslaught upon the hordes of Asia. Go where you will, study the reasons of the rise and fall of nations, and the most potent of them will be found in the fact of their recognition or ignoring of the God who made them, and His commandments.

There never was a community, from that Friday evening when, in darkness, in cold, and in storm, its founders groped upon Clark's Island, until the present, in the which God and His word have been more profoundly revered; and never, from the foundation of the world, has a community exerted so wide-spread and benign an influence for pure religion as has this. But I hear you say, "Our townsmen and kinsmen, — tell us of them." The story is not a long one.

Aug. 11, 1798, In a cottage still standing in yonder hamlet of Stony Brook, the twins, Charles and Ichabod, were born. Their mother, sixth in descent from the first Gov. Bradford, was left a widow in six months from that time, and hard was the struggle this devoted mother had, to cherish these two boys and the older sister into self-sustaining maturity.

Ichabod was early apprenticed to a blacksmith near the city of Worcester, and from that time until his death in 1870, his life was a constant experience of intelligent industry and self-culture rewarded with success; and to-day the manufacturing house founded by his skill, and bearing his name is much the largest in the city of his adoption; and in that same city are flourishing four great charities originated, and wholly or in part endowed by him, which will ever cause his name to be remembered with gratitude.

Charles fitted for Brown University under "Parson Willis," whose cottage we passed this morning, was graduated in 1820, studied law in Norway, Me., married the daughter of the first county justice before whom he tried a case; lived and practised in that State until 1837, when he moved to Worcester with his family, and joined fortunes with his brother Ichabod. His death occurred in October last.

The affection subsisting between these brothers was always marked. They loved to refer to themselves as "twins." They lived side by side in Worcester the last half of their lives. As before intimated, a frequent subject of conversation between them was "Old Kingston" and the friends and experiences of their young days. Among others, the fact that Charles, when fitting for college, "watched" in the old woolen mill on Jones River, just south of Kingston Village, and that Ichabod often cheered the lonely vigils of his brother, was often discussed by them. This phase of their young lives is referred to in some lines read by a member of the family at a dinner celebrating their seventieth birthday, and there is so much in them significant of the fraternal sympathy that always subsisted between them, and there are so many present who are deeply interested in everything connected with the brothers, that I will venture to read them.

> The sunset rays had faded,
>   The sky had lost its light,
> Its starry diadem lit up
>   The dusky brow of Night.
>
> The busy wheel hangs motionless,
>   The waters ripple by,
> No sound disturbs the stillness,
>   No living thing is nigh,
>
> Save a little, lonely figure,
>   The watchman of the mill;
> Whose quiet footfall breaketh
>   The silence deep and still,
>
> As he paced with childish footsteps
>   The old brown walls about,
> And watched the stars till daylight
>   As they one by one went out.
>
> He keeps his lonely vigil
>   With a faithful, earnest heart,
> Though weariness assails him
>   As the lengthening hours depart.

And he walks the dark old chambers
  In silence and alone,
While the light of a little lantern
  About his footsteps shone.

The sighing wind in the forest
  Stirs his boyish heart with fear,
And he hears with a chill of terror
  A footstep drawing near.

Straight up the rocky pathway,
  Onward, right on, it came;
A voice breaks the evening stillness,
  It calls him by his name.

An answering cry burst from him;
  He knew his brother's call,
And sprang with joy to meet him
  In the shade of the ancient wall.

" Why come you here," he questions,
  " At this lonely hour of night,
When to labor you must hasten
  With the earliest dawn of light?"

" I could not rest, dear brother,"
  The elder one replied.
" You slept not on my pillow,
  I missed you from my side.

" Let me stay with you, brother,
  While you your vigil keep;
The thought of your lonely hours
  Would haunt me in my sleep."

The little watchman answered,
  As he heard his loving prayer,
" The lonely hours too short would seem,
  Did you my watching share.

" I cannot work like you, brother,
  For this we often grieve,"—
And the eyes of both glanced downward
  At a little empty sleeve,—

"But a brave, stout heart I have, brother,
    My duty I will do,
And when I need two hands in toil,
    Why, then I'll lean on you."

So faithfully they labored,
    Each one his place to fill;
They worked at the forge and anvil,
    And watched in the old brown mill.

Life's pathway lay before them,
    Its rugged steeps untrod;
Unaided they must tread it,
    Save by their father — God.

With strong, brave hearts they struggled
    Manfully side by side;
While years passed swiftly o'er them,
    And blessings multiplied.

Though in toil and many a hardship
    Their lot was often cast,
In mutual love and sympathy
    Boyhood and youth were passed.

When many years of manhood
    Had tinged their locks with gray,
God's finger touched the elder;
    He faltered by the way.

While the nights were long and weary,
    And his listless hands lay still,
He dreamed of the scenes of childhood,
    And the nights in the old brown mill.

Though the faith and hope of the Christian
    Shone bright in this trial hour,
The love that blessed his boyhood
    Had never lost its power.

When strength ebbed low within him,
    And the lamp of life burned dim,
He could not leave his brother
    While he had need of him.

So he struggled up from the river,
   Though lingering long on the brink,
And once and again of its waters
   His lips were pressed to drink.

He had deemed the battle over,
   He thought his life-work done;
That the soldier's watch was ended
   And the rest of the Christian won.

But another year these brothers
   Are lingering on the shore.
To celebrate their natal day
   We now return once more.

The friends with whom in former days
   The path of life they trod,
Are gathering, a family,
   About the throne of God.

Bright angels safely guide them
   As they cross life's troubled sea,
And reach that quiet haven,
   From pain and sorrow free!

The love they bear each other
   As brightly glows to-day
As when in hours of infancy
   They in one cradle lay.

So at the last sad moment,
   When parting words are spoken,
May they cross the shining river
   With the mystic tie unbroken!

                                M. E. W.

AUGUST 11, 1868.

My friends, I will not detain you longer. Many and affectionate are the personal greetings my father and uncle would give if they were here! I, in their behalf, now thank the warm hearts of Kingston for the many kind words and expressions with which they followed these brothers as long as they lived, and let me assure you that they were always appreciated. For myself, let me beg you, young and old, cherish the hearthstones of Old Kingston. Do not forget your past, so peculiar, simple, perhaps, in detail, but so grand in its results! As the children grow up, repeat to them the precious associations of Plymouth and Kingston, that they, as thousands before them have, may in turn transplant into the regions, north, west, and south of our dear country, the practice of those virtues which have given this portion of the Old Colony the world-wide name and prase it now enjoys.

---

14. The son of Kingston who has the most relatives, good, bad, and indifferent, " Uncle Cook."

TO HAVE BEEN RESPONDED TO BY RUFUS R. COOK, ESQ, OF BOSTON.

Much regret has been felt and expressed that at least a few moments could not have been allowed for speaking at the table, to this energetic and philanthropic son of the town. The thoughts that were prompted by the occasion, he assures us, could not after a few weeks be gathered up or put into the form of a speech by his pen.

Mr. Cook has for years been chaplain of the Suffolk County Jail, and has been " the prisoner's friend" in the municipal court-room of Boston.

In many instances he gives his personal bond for the reappearance of those arraigned and for their good behavior for a definite period. Through his kind and Christian influence, many of the fallen have been reclaimed, and the number of the vicious has been reduced. Believing in the old doctrine that prevention is better than cure, he has labored assiduously to promote the cause of temperance and also has bestowed his energies for the salvation of the young in Sabbath Schools.

He has thus fairly earned the enviable distinction of a universal uncle, finding warm friends among all classes, conditions, and ages.

The above statement having been submitted to one of the justices of the Municipal Court (Hon. Mr. Chamberlain), he says, "It is both accurate and just. Indeed, it is hardly possible to overestimate the importance of the work Mr. Cook has undertaken, and for years has quietly pursued, and his admirable fitness for it. He is so constant in his attendance upon the court that my associates and myself have come to regard him as one of its officers, and he is never absent without being missed. The city has few better or more useful men than "Uncle Cook."

---

15. Rhode Island and Delaware, States almost too small to contain the Works of two Kingston boys, whom we are happy to number among our honored Vice-Presidents to-day.

RESPONDED TO FIRST, BY HON. GEORGE B. HOLMES, OF PROVIDENCE, R. I.

Mr. President, — In response to a sentiment referring to Rhode Island, I have to say that, although I am a Rhode Islander by an adoption of half a century, I still remember with pride that Kingston is the town of my birth. Here I passed the pleasant days of childhood and youth. I remember, with a feeling of gratitude, that when only twenty-six years of age, I was elected from this town as a member of the State Convention for the revision of the Constitution in 1820, and had the privilege of listening to the debates of the eminent men who belonged to that body, upon the fundamental law. My election was rather singular. I was not nominated or even asked, neither did I know I was to be voted for, nor did I attend the town-meeting; but a friend called on me in the evening and gave me the information. I attended the Convention, and it was a very great help to me. My political course was then changed, and I have not entered into the political field since, very strongly. During the attendance of the Convention, I became fully convinced that all governments are controlled by a Divine Providence, and my duty was to vote for the best man.

As all men, whether exiles by compulsion or chance, constantly recall with satisfaction the just renown of their native place, so it has always been with me an unfailing source of pleasure to dwell upon the reputation, which my old home has acquired for solid worth and the prevalence of those substantial virtues, which are at once the strength and glory of the individual and national life. I refer to official and private honesty, strict regard for confided trusts, thrift, temperance, and intelligence. If Kingston has not risen to commercial empire, like New York or Boston, she has, nevertheless, the satisfaction of knowing that she has avoided the questionable blessing of great debts and town bonds, and that in that greatness which is the final salvation of all countries, the greatness of a thrifty, patriotic, and moral citizenship, she is far more opulent than she would be with a harbor filled with fleets of merchantmen, and with warehouses groaning under the product of every clime.

But fond as I am of the reputation of my native town and State, I am yet equally fond of the reputation of my adopted home, in whose behalf I am invited to speak. I remained in Kingston till July, 1824, when I moved to Providence and entered into the foundry and machine business. I have had the management of this business almost fifty-two years. Our establishment was at first small, but with the growth of our city, which has gone up from 20,000 to 108,000 in population, the business has very naturally increased from a capital of $14,000 to $300,000. Though I have five times been elected a member of the General Assembly of my adopted State, I have never entered very deeply into politics. Business has been my hobby, and of course, in a State so small in territory as your toast intimates, our Works occupy a larger space comparatively than if they had been in Massachusetts.

But Rhode Island, small as she is, has innumerable voices to speak for her. Her enterprise is known of all men; her patriotism sealed with blood; her piety written in letters of devotion and death on many missionary fields; her scholarship ripening in harvests of learning in every State of the Union; her courage proved on a hundred battle-fields, flashing in the light of the burning "Gaspee," heralded by the flying splinters from Perry's frigate, and consecrated by the dying gallantry of Slocum and Rodman, and a host of unrecorded heroes, — these all speak for Rhode Island. And in the great struggle for commercial renown her success has not been less distinguished. Let her million spindles, her pattern-cards displayed in every market, her toiling engines moving the universal wheels of industry, be her sufficient eulogists.

My hope and my prayer is that to her, as to that place of my childhood so fondly cherished, God may grant deliverance from past error and misfortune, and may give countless centuries of prosperity in the future. And finally, as for myself, it being more than fifty years since I left Kingston, my experience of life has been varied and continued beyond the time ordinarily vouchsafed to man.

Among life's chances a return to Kingston, to rest my dying eyes upon her green fields and to lie down among my ancestors, will probably not be granted me; but I trust that a kind Providence will grant me beyond the grave an existence, where the memory of her green fields and quiet streams will not be taken from me.

RESPONDED TO ALSO BY LETTER FROM GEORGE G. LOBDELL, ESQ., OF WILMINGTON, DEL.

WILMINGTON, DEL., June 22, 1876.

Dear Sir, — Yours of the 5th inst. to "Hon. George G. Lobdell" was duly received. As there are no persons of the name in this section, other than my own family, I suppose it was intended for me. Although I have something of a national reputation with railroad men, as a manufacturer of railroad wheels and the inventor of the first plate railroad-wheel which was a success, I have never filled any political position entitling me to the prefix of "Honorable," and have never had any ambition in that direction, neither am I given to making speeches; therefore I could not reply to one of your toasts. However, if I could do so, it would afford me great pleasure to visit Kingston and participate in the proposed celebration, and to have accompany me some who are not only proud of the name of Blue Hens' Chickens, but boast also that they can trace their genealogy to the Pilgrims, — Elder Brewster, Thomas Prince, Philip de la Noye, Edward Bompasse, and through their mother to Peregrine White.

I find, however, that I cannot leave home on account of the Centennial Exhibition, having with us several friends, and I am expecting others to attend this, the most wonderful exhibit that the world ever produced. We have been notified that our Works, which are the oldest and I believe the largest of the kind in the country, will be visited by several of the commissions of foreign countries, which, taken with the fact that I shall have to meet the judges on a part of our exhibits on the 27th inst., will prevent my leaving home during this month.

Yours very respectfully,

GEORGE G. LOBDELL.

16. Letter from Ex.-Gov. Emory Washburn to an invitation to be present and to participate in the exercises.

CAMBRIDGE, June 10, 1876.

Gentlemen, — Your favor of the 5th inst., extending to me a flattering invitation to be present at the celebration of the citizens of Kingston on the 27th inst., reached me as I was starting for New York, too late to reply to it then, and I seize the first moment after my return to thank you for the honor you have done me, and to express my sincere regret that, as our Commencement comes on the 28th, I cannot with any propriety be absent from my place here on the preceding day. I shall greatly regret to lose the pleasure of being present where there will be so much to enjoy, and shall be sorry to lose, moreover, an opportunity to renew my claim, as I do on all proper occasions, to being of the Old Colony lineage, though my birthplace, without any choice on my part, happened to be within the limits of Massachusetts Bay. If I cannot go back quite to the Mayflower, I claim relationship with Plymouth Rock, as my line of descent goes back to a granddaughter of Mary Chilton; and as Kingston was a daughter of Plymouth, if I could have been present on the commemoration of her birth-day, I should have put in my claim, with much pride and satisfaction, of having come to a family gathering and having my heirship recognized.

I am sorry to lose the chance of having my hereditary rank recognized, but shall try to content myself with the honor of having been invited to participate on that occasion with so many, of whose appreciation I should be justly proud.

Very respectfully, your ob't servant,
EMORY WASHBURN.

17. Our Native Town :

> "'Mid pleasures and palaces though we may roam,
> Be it ever so humble, there's no place like home."

RESPONDED TO BY DR. FREDERIC W. BARTLETT, OF BUFFALO, NEW YORK.

Mr. President, Ladies and Gentlemen, — I am invited to respond to this sentiment, and I do so with pleasure. In all ages and all nations, the love of home has been a dominant feeling of the human heart. Even the inhabitant of cheerless, frozen Iceland considers it the "best land on which the sun shines," and

> " The naked negro panting at the line
> Boasts of his golden skies and palmy wine."

If the love of home cannot be stifled in the breasts of these unfortunates, how shall one born in this lovely town ever become insensible to its marvellous attractions? For it is the

> " Sweet Auburn! *loveliest* village of the plain,"

of all the smiling hamlets peacefully scattered over our grand, historic State, with motherly Plymouth sending forth the bold headlands of Manomet, and the Gurnet to resist the rudeness of the storm-swept ocean, and Jones River flowing, a ribbon of silver, from its source to the embrace of the quiet bay, winding and hesitating as if reluctant to leave such tranquil scenes, and beyond the bay with the noble hill, home of the great military leader, Standish, with Monk's Hill on the south, and all the lakes, each with tiny streamlet to carry its surplus to swell the volume of the gently-flowing river. I doubt if there is a finer panoramic view in all this fair land than that from Abraham's

Hill. Here, too, are the memorials of those who gave birth to this great nation. It seems incredible that within the scope of our vision lived the people who organized government by the people, and gave to this land all that is valuable in its institutions. We may criticise their weaknesses, but dare we, as a people, in a political or religious sense, prefer any just claim to superiority? I am proud of this town for its noble record in all those qualities which make a people truly great, proud of the patriotism which has given our bravest and best for the defence of liberty and law, and I remember with pathetic tenderness all those who on land or sea have yielded up their lives for their country. "They sleep for the flag; and may the light of its glorious stars shed pleasant dreams upon their loyal souls forever!"

No town on all the coast has furnished better qualified commanders in the merchant marine than Adams, Symmes, Holmes, and Baker; and no river of its size has witnessed the launching of so many noble vessels by Holmes, Sever, and others, whose sails have whitened and keels made musical the most distant waters of the globe.

I am grateful to Almighty God that my birth was in this upright, moral, Christian community; that in all my boyhood years no licensed or unlicensed temptation lured me to drunkenness or immorality; for its good schools, with such teachers as Jason Winnett, David Thayer, and Hollis Stone. I am proud of the thrift and honesty which in a population of 1,700 has but one individual in its almshouse to-day. This community has always cheered its sons in every good work, and no one need ever fear an envious disparagement of his success; on the contrary, he may be assured that every stride he may make to eminence, wealth, or fame will be mentioned with satisfaction by all his townsmen. The allurements of the great world outside have taken many of your sons to other and distant scenes, but the old love remains, and is well expressed by Goldsmith in these familiar lines: —

> "In all my wanderings round this world of care,
> In all my griefs, — and God has given my share, —
> I still had hopes my latest hours to crown,
> Amidst these humble bowers to lay me down;
> To husband out life's taper at the close,
> And keep the flame from wasting by repose.
> I still had hopes — for pride attends us still —
> Amidst the swains to show my book-learned skill;
> Around my fire an evening group to draw,
> And tell of all I felt and all I saw;
> And, as a hare whom hounds and horns pursue,
> Pants to the place from whence at first she flew,
> I still had hopes, my long vexations passed,
> Here to return — and die at home at last."

I do not recall an instance in all my boyhood of a conviction for crime of a native of this community.

Good Justice Eli Cook had always a dry inkstand, and the exotics whose pleasantries he punished, came like celestial visitors, "few and far between."

There were jovial little coteries of village statesmen at the shop of Joseph Stetson (a most excellent and useful citizen, whom I regret is physically unable to be here to-day), but in all their discussions, no matter how animated, I do not remember to have listened to profanity. You have good homes, good municipal regulations, and are given to kindly sympathy for each other in sickness or other adversity. Your religious teachers have been men of culture and unsullied character, considerate and friendly and tolerant of the views of others.

> "Peace be within your borders, and prosperity within your gates!"

Cling to the grand old principles which you glorify in your ancestors. Protect the youth of to-day, as our fathers protected us, by a steadfast opposition to concessions to vice in every form. Let them safely walk these streets, and give them those elements of character which alone can achieve success. May it be truly said of us, and all of us, that we are faithful to high responsibilities. And so, as Tiny Tim observed, "God bless us, every one!"

---

18. Kingston Inventions.

SPEECH BY T. D. STETSON, ESQ., OF NEW YORK CITY.

The old mode of boring holes in wood was by a pod-auger, which had to be drawn out at intervals to empty the pod. Now we bore continuously through two feet or more of dense timber in ship and bridge work, and the chips are worked out as fast as cut. This is the result of the introduction of the screw-auger. John Washburn, of Kingston, Mass., was the inventor in the latter part of the last century. He also invented cut nails and tacks. He cut the blanks in one machine, and employed children to pick them up one by one with their fingers, and insert them in the places where they were to be headed.

Jesse Reed, then of Kingston, put the improvement upon that which made it a commercial success. He held the blank by a spring after it was cut, and by the motion of the cutting knife itself moved it into the dies and left it there. He made the cutting and heading one operation, and ever since his Kingston patents of 1809–10–11, the nail machine has been able to take in plate iron at one point, and drop the finished nail or tack at another, at the rate of about three per second, till the knives or dies become dull and require a delay of ten minutes for grinding. The screw-auger, the cut nail, and the machine for making the cut nail, are all Kingston inventions.

Kingston, with a population of less than 2,000, — one twenty-thousandth part of the American Union, — has done her full share to promote the present advanced condition of the arts. None of Kingston's sons have as yet made fortunes by their inventions without work, but with the same great strides, or even with much smaller ones, the chances are far greater for doing it now than a century ago. They are still at work. The patent is only a few years old on an improvement in stump pullers, one of the first necessities for backwoods' farming, invented by Caleb Bates or Thomas Newcomb, or both, and forged by Christopher Drew with the water power of Stony Brook, which flows past the Kingston depot. These are all residents and active business men of Kingston. The railroad is, on the other hand, a type and a product of the most rapid and dashing civilization. Our railroad cars glide over long lines of steel rails on our Western prairies, and move through the rocky defiles of our sister republics in South America, on wheels containing improvements invented and patented by George G. Lobdell, a native of Kingston, and manufactured in a large way in Wilmington, Del., by a company of which he is the head.

It is hard to conceive anything more simple than an invention of Martin Washburn, of Kingston, not yet patented, for cleaning horses, or anything more abstruse and intangible than the invention of Dr. Frederic W. Bartlett, one of Kingston's sons, practising medicine in Buffalo, which has just been patented here and in Europe. He makes ozone better. Ozone is electrified oxygen, electrified water, oxide of oxygen, double oxygen, peroxide of hydrogen, the bleaching principle of chlorine, the disinfecting, vitalizing, purifying principle of fresh-burned charcoal, or of nature generally. Nobody knows what it is as well as he does nails and augers, but Dr. Bartlett knows what is of more importance practically, — how to make it, — and his invention is attracting much attention in scientific societies. Heretofore ozone could be made artificially, but too impure. Instead of pleasing, it offended; instead of invigorating, it choked. The Bartlett process promises to give, at a practicable cost, a useful gas, destined, it is hoped, to become, like ice and chloroform, a necessity in every hospital.

Kingston inventors have made probably their proportion of failures. Osborne Morton and Asaph Holmes, of Kingston, labored together, twenty years or more ago, to attain perpetual motion, or something which cannot be much distinguished from it. Their faith was too great. But another Kingston inventor, a half century earlier, nearly attained one of the most successful machines, in a pecuniary sense, in the world, — the harvesting machine. No one, until Obed Hussey, in 1833, made a useful invention in that line; but Samuel Adams, of Kingston, made one of the early attempts, and went all the way to Washington on horseback to obtain a patent, which issued Dec. 28, 1805. The records have been burned, but it is believed to have been close in the line of the present machine, which has contributed millions to the wealth of individuals, and hundreds of millions to our nation's greatness and to the prosperity of the world. His faith was too weak.

Unsuccessful experiments do not benefit the world, and are no longer cited in the courts to defeat patents. They tend to establish, so far as they establish anything, that success in that direction is impossible. They signal to keep off, rather than to follow. But it is hard if we try, which we will not, to avoid a deep feeling of sympathy for the luckless toiler in the mine of invention, who, through want of merit in his conception, or through want of capital, persistence, or judgment in developing it, almost, but not quite, succeeds. Success is not in obtaining a patent, — many other Kingston men have reached that point, — but in making the invention useful and profitable. The United States Lock Company, now manufacturing at Kingston, make probably the very best lock in the world, but the invention is not by a citizen or native of Kingston; so I will not dwell on it.

John Washburn did not try to keep secret, or to patent, or in any other way to protect his inventions. He threw them out for any to copy, — just as he did his successful adoption of previous foreign arts, in the casting of sleigh-bells with the balls magically contained inside, and just as his brother, Elisha Washburn (my grandfather), did with the model and details of the construction of the famous Kingston fishing-boat, "Moll Corey," which it was the ambition of fisherman and fancy sailors vainly to try to equal fifty years ago.

As the law and practice now stands, nearly every really important forward step in the arts can be protected for the exclusive benefit of the originator for a considerable term, either by patent for invention, patent for design, or by registration of trade-mark, or by copyright; and it is every one's duty, to himself and family, to avail himself of the privilege, when he makes a happy hit.

I have used names, and spoken them plainly out loud, and it is right. It is an American weakness to glorify Americans generally and decry or ignore them specifically. An inventor, artist, or *savant* is fortunate who is born in England. The English praise Englishmen, Americans copy from English books; and the science of Newton and Brewster, the pictures of Turner and Landseer, and the inventions of Watt, Hargreaves, and Bessamer are famous wherever the English language is spoken. Let us not refuse to the past or to the present inventions of our countrymen and our neighbors the credit of distinct public acknowledgement, which is in too many cases the only reward.

———

19. The celebration of our anniversary abundantly pays in the privilege it affords of reunion after years of separation, to those who once were boys of our schools and at play around the old hearth-stones of their native town.

RESPONDED TO BY RICHARD HOLMES, ESQ., OF BOSTON.

Mr. President, Ladies and Gentlemen, — After listening to the highly interesting remarks of the gentlemen who have preceded me, I should not presume to occupy a moment of your time, were it not for the fact that I should prove recreant to the promptings of my own heart if I did not here, in the home of my nativity, surrounded by so many friends of my youth, promptly respond to your call, if it were merely to express to you, sir, and these friends, the strong attachment that I still have for the good old town within whose limits I passed sweet childhood's happy days. I have learned from observation, Mr. President, that this strong attachment for early home is a characteristic somewhat peculiar to New Englanders; for in my travels in the Western States, where I have been brought in contact with many settlers who went out from New England, I have ever found predominant in their affections, this reverential love for early home; and rare, very rare, have been the instances where they were not anticipating with pleasure the time when they should return to pass their declining years upon or near to the old homestead. I am confident, Mr. President, that many within the sound of my voice will bear testimony to the fact that, although many, very many links in the chain of early affections may have been severed, and many new associations formed, yet wherever or whatever may be the home of our adoption, there ever linger in our memories sweet reminiscences of the dear old home; and though many of the transactions of recent life may have passed into oblivion, vivid in our recollections are the scenes of our youthful days. I am truly grateful, Mr. President, that you have, in the exercise of your judgment, assigned to me the duty of responding to the sentiment commemorative of early days and of the pleasure of our reunion; for on this, the one hundred and fiftieth birthday of the town which you and I, sir, have ever been proud to call our home, standing on the turf that my youthful feet so often trod, with so many suggestive surroundings, it would be impossible for me to give utterance to sentiments other than those pertaining to the old home and the scenes of my boyhood. Well do we remember, as though it were but yesterday, when, in the days of Samuel Glover and John Allen (worthy representatives of both of whom I am happy to greet here to-day), we, each Sabbath morning, with Sunday-school books in hand, marched up this dusty road to the old Baptist Church (an edifice to us then so sanctified, now somewhat demoralized); and after listening to the pious instructions of the morning from the sacred desk and repeating our well-studied verses in the Sabbath School, how hugely we enjoyed the hour spent in the woods, upon the river's bank, or in gathering berries, which, notwithstanding the pious injunctions of the morning, we deemed no sacrilege as long as they were needed for home consumption! Returning to the church in the afternoon, how nobly we struggled to divert our minds from the woods, the river, and the berries, which we had so reluctantly left, in order that we might take in sufficient religious instruction to keep us well balanced until the succeeding Sabbath! I confess, Mr. President, that in the exuberance of our youthfulness, it sometimes scarcely lasted, but in the emergency, the admonitions received under the paternal roof and the discipline of the school-teacher performed wonders in making good the void.

I see many before me to whom it is unnecessary to recount the experience of the old red school-house or the circumstances attending our early scholarship, for in our spelling-matches, our struggles for the supremacy in mathematics and other kindred studies, as well as in the enjoyment of the truant hour and the participation in the punishment so sure to follow, they were ever the sharers of my joys and sorrows, and although we never professed to believe in the old adage, "Stolen fruit is ever the sweetest;" when the favorite apple and pear became palatable we were never defaulted, but ready to put in an appearance at the right time. How enjoyable were our excursions to Monks' Hill, Smelt Pond, Billington Sea, and other favorite kindred localities! How pleasant our fishing and sailing excursions in the harbor, which usually ended with a fish chowder at the Gurnet, or a clam chowder on White Flat, none the less palatable because they were prepared by our own hands. Indelibly stamped upon our memories are the minutest transactions of our youth, and as we here recount them this thought is suggested: The companions of our youth, — where are they? Some of them, true to home attachments, have remained here to make good the places of our fathers and sustain the character and standing of the good old town (for which they are worthy of commendation); others have located in neighboring cities and towns of the commonwealth; still others have sought their fortunes in a more distant clime; while many, very many, Mr. President, have passed on to a higher life; and whether their bodies are deposited with our fathers in yonder consecrated ground or repose on some distant shore, I make no doubt they are with us in spirit to-day, participating in our enjoyments, and that we shall by this social gathering, aided by their influences, become holier, happier, better.

Mr. President, at this fraternal reunion, while I would not bring the tear to a single eye, or cast the faintest shadow over this joyous gathering, in tribute to those who have gone before us I give you as a sentiment: *The memory of our loved ones.* And by your permission and the indulgence of these kind friends, I will recite a few lines that I trust on this occasion will not be deemed inappropriate.

>From busy care, at close of day,
> How sweet to steal an hour away!
>   Where'er in life we roam.
> And, free from trouble, noise, and strife,
> Reflect on scenes of early life,
>   With thoughts of dear old home.
> The village school, where by us stood
> Companions ever true and good,
> With teachers kind, who in their vocation
> Maintained the honors of their station;
> The churches, all so reverent dressed
> That each one deemed their church the best;
> The men of God, who from sacred desk
> Proclaimed the danger and the risk
> If Satan's shafts were not defied,
> While they preached to us Christ crucified;
> The pleasant woods and lovely grove,
> Where we with dear ones oft did rove!
> The dear old fields and gurgling brooks,
> Upon whose banks in shady nooks,
> By subtile and deceptive plan,
> Practised too oft by artful man,
> We lured the guileless, speckled trout,
> And as he took our bait *in* we took him *out*.
> When these old scenes to mind are brought
> We bless our memory for the thought;
> And for pleasant woods and bounding sea,
> Each flowering shrub and towering tree,
> For meadows green and meandering river,
> Grateful are we to God, the Giver.
> As we these scenes to mind recall
> There comes one thought dearer than all;
> And in that thought you all will share, —
> 'T is of a mother's love, a father's care.

> These priceless gems cannot be bought;
> And 't is our noblest, sweetest thought,
> That whether by land or sea we roam,
> We ne 'er forget our parents' home.
> And as they pass on, their children's love
> They bear with them to that home above;
>   And though by us unseen,
> We 'll cherish in our heart of hearts,
> Lives ever true in all their parts,
>   And keep their memory green.

---

20. The fair daughters of Kingston. Who will not speak for them impromptu?

A LETTER FROM MRS. E. M. C. WALSH.

PHILADELPHIA, June 23, 1876.

MESSRS. STETSON, WILLIS, PECKHAM, BARTLETT, AND OTHERS:

Gentlemen, — While I regret that circumstances will prevent my being present at the festivities attendant on the celebration of the one hundred and fiftieth anniversary of dear old Kingston as an incorporated town, allow me to thank you for your kind remembrance after so long an absence from the home of my childhood. I have read and re-read the old familiar names, and they have brought back to my mind scenes and events of earlier years until I have almost seemed young again. I love my dear native place, its very name sends a throb of joy to my heart. May God's blessings be ever above and around it! is the sincere wish of

        Yours truly,

           ELIZA M. CHANDLER WALSH.

VOLUNTEER TOASTS.

1. The Union, established by deeds of valor and cemented by the blood of the heroes of the Revolution, North, South, East, and West. May it endure forever!

BY PHILANDER COBB, ESQ.

---

2. Kingston, always lovingly remembered by her dutiful children, whether at home or abroad.

BY ALDEN SAMPSON, ESQ., CHARLESTOWN, MASS.

---

3. Jones River. Though unknown in song and story, with no foreign keels plowing its "short reach," yet its staunch fleets have reached every foreign shore.

---

4. The clam banks of our bay. Their welcome currency relieved our fathers in their sorest depression; their rich issues rule the market in town and city to-day.

BY CAPT. FRANK A. JAMESON.

POEM BY GEORGE C. BURGESS.

Mr. President, Fellow-Citizens, — I had hoped to be spared
From answering to a toast to-day, for I'm wholly unprepared!
I knew, to be of Pilgrim blood, you held as proudest boast,
And so I thought you too *well-bred* for making up a *toast*.
I've listened well to that address which told us so much new
About old times, and wondered not that it attention *Drew*.
The *ring* of eloquent words we know from a full heart must spring,
But when it's not political, we all do *Love (a) ring*.
With martial strain and soldiers' tread and childhood's smiling face,
We joined in dusty march to-day to find this resting-place;
Imagination's magic wand it was that showed the way —
I'm sure 'twas *Fa(u)nce's* form I saw, who led us here to-day.
And as our first man *Adams* here, we ought, I do believe,
Though it would keep us five hours more, we ought to wait for *eve*.
I thought, as back to the old times our minds to-day were drawn,
And of the full centennial we dwelt upon its dawn,
And praised with no unstinted speech the words and deeds so bold
That through a hundred years and more, have undiminished rolled,
And thanked our stars whose influence had made our fathers thus,

What if the years could be rolled back, *what would they think of us!*
You all have seen a telescope, a tube with glass and things,
You put the small end to your eye, and close at hand it brings
Whatever object you may wish its wondrous power to try.
But turn the instrument about, how far those objects fly!
We all of us to-day have gazed away down in the past,
And through time's telescope our gaze with lingering looks have cast,
But as we used the smaller lens and scanned their actions all,
They'll have to use the larger one, and *would n't we look small!*
And yet it is n't quite unmixed, this feeling of respect,
Unless we're filled with Pilgrim blood, and sit with the elect.
I've a young couple in my eye, I scorn to make them blush,
Who think some old-time Pilgrim laws not worth a single rush.
You ask me why? The reason's plain, for in those laws is laid
A fine of twenty shillings due if man shall kiss a maid.
And every woman here will say in some things they were wrong,
When they forbade that any wear a ribbon two yards long;
And many a man would hesitate to give some laws good heed,
For stocks and fines awaited those who used the soothing weed.
While children meditate, no doubt, upon the improved plan
By which the restless ones at church escape " ye tythinge mann."
And yet with all their uncouth ways, we feel a pride to-day,
That faithless men and adverse winds drove them to Plymouth Bay.
As the rough chestnut's fruit, whose burr, so hard and sharp to hold,
Does in its inmost heart, so soft, the kernel sweet enfold.
'Neath rudest dress and roughest words, they hid the truest heart,
That deep within its tenderness of God's love held a part.
And fellow-citizens, this toast I beg to give to all, —
God grant *our* memories fragrant live the *next* centennial!

MAP OF KINGSTON.

THE new and enlarged map of the town and village of Kingston which accompanies this volume has been prepared with much care and cost, and is invaluable as a present directory and guide; but it is coupled with the pamphlet account of the late celebration for two important reasons: first, as setting forth in a sensible manner a sort of summary of two and a half centuries' progress since the first settlement of the town; and second, as affording the ready means to those who shall come after us for ascertaining its condition in this commemorative year of our national independence, 1876. Soon the things that *are* will be among the things that *were*, and the facts hereby presented will become important and permanent history. Having so recently felt the great need of just such information in respect to the former and ancient inhabitants, the location of their dwellings, schoolhouses, mills, roads, and bridges, it becomes no less our pleasure than duty to put these matters upon enduring tablets for the benefit of generations yet to come. We hereby discharge one of the debts we owe to posterity.

CONTENTS.

Extracts from Archives of Massachusetts relating to Kingston . 117
Historical Sketch by T. B. Drew 43
Hymn by Mrs. C. B. Burgess 15
Hymn by T. B. Drew 12
Introduction 5
Letter of Francis D. Bartlett 94
Letter of George G. Lobdell 136
Letter of John T. Prince 95
Letter of George B. Robbins 95
Letter of Frank J. Symmes 96
Letter of Albert Stetson 94
Letter of Winslow W. Sever 110
Letter of Mrs. E. M. C. Walsh 149
Letter of Emory Washburn 137
Notice of R. R. Cook 132
Notice of Speech of Henry B. Peirce 69
Notice of Town Map 151
Officers of the Day 3
Oration by Rev. Joseph F. Lovering 17
Poems by George C. Burgess 38, 150
Speech of Nathaniel Adams 11
Speech of Ellis Ames 97
Speech of Frederick W. Bartlett 138
Speech of Joseph R. Chandler 73
Speech of John B. D. Cogswell 112
Speech of Wm. T. Davis 70
Speech of William A. Drew 83
Speech of George B. Holmes 133
Speech of Richard Holmes 145
Speech of Francis M. Johnson 107
Speech of George B. Loring 64
Speech of Thomas D. Stetson 141
Speech of Edward S. Tobey 67
Speech and Poem of Charles F. Washburn 125
Speech and Poems of Henry S. Washburn 118
Volunteer Toasts 150

REPORT

OF THE

Proceedings and Exercises

AT THE

CELEBRATION

OF THE

ONE HUNDRED AND FIFTIETH ANNIVERSARY

OF THE

Incorporation of the Town of Kingston, Mass.,

June 27, 1876.

BOSTON:
E. B. STILLINGS & CO., PRINTERS, 15 Spring Lane.
1876.

Printed in Dunstable, United Kingdom